KNITTING
with Kate O'Brien

D0452741

GILL AND MACMILLAN
and
RADIO TELEFÍS ÉIREANN

Published by
Gill and Macmillan Ltd
Goldenbridge
Dublin 8
and
Radio Telefís Éireann
Donnybrook
Dublin 4
© Kate O'Brien 1990
0 7171 1814 2
Edited by Roberta Reeners
Designed by Design Image, Dublin
Colour Photography - Walter Pfeiffer Studios, Dublin
Black and White Photography - Joe Geoghegan Studios, Galway
Models' Make-Up - Fiona Cannon
Hair by Karen of David Marshall Studios
Colour origination by Kulor Centre Ltd
Printed by Criterion Press, Dublin

Last copy

To William O'Brien, the artist, and to Margaret Kidd, the expert knitter who taught me everything in this book and more.

ACKNOWLEDGMENTS

Special thanks to Noel and Brid Flavin of Needlecraft for their help and encouragement over the past four years as well as their assistance with this book. John Cashell of Tivoli deserves most sincere thanks for his generous assistance. Thanks are also due to my editor, Roberta Reeners, and the team at Design Image for their endless patience.

Finally, thanks so much to the following:

Pat Kelly for achieving the Improbable;

Elizabeth Molony, Anne Conway and Louise O'Brien for their unique brand of sanity, infinite analysis, good humour and food in adversity;

The 'Live at 3' team for putting up with a lunatic for four long years and remaining uncorrupted.

CONTENTS

❖ ❖ ❖ ❖
1. CHOOSING THE RIGHT FIBRES

❖ ❖ ❖ ❖
Yarns

Yarns may be defined as threads which have been specially spun for knitting into finished garments. The thread may be hand or machine spun and made of cotton, linen, silk, wool or other animal fibres. Always choose your yarns carefully, keeping in mind the type of garment you wish to make.

❖ ❖ ❖ ❖
Cottons

Cotton yarn is produced from the ripe, fluffy seed pod of the cotton plant. It is cool, strong, easy to wash and absorbent. It is therefore extremely pleasant to wear. There are three basic types of cotton yarn.

1. *'Spun' natural (or 'raw') cotton*
   This is good, inexpensive and hard wearing.

2. *'Slub' cotton*
   This has a 'thick-and-thin' appearance. It is sometimes called 'bouclé' yarn. It has a nice, soft texture and is very sporty and casual.

3. *'Mercerized' cotton*
   This has a shiny, pearly appearance. It has been specially treated to prevent piling and shredding and to ensure that it will retain its silky appearance.

❖ ❖ ❖ ❖
Linen

Linen is spun from the fibrous stalks of the flax plant. It is extremely tough, absorbent and cool to wear. Its strength actually increases with washing. It is because of this quality that it was once used for sheets and other household linens such as tablecloths. Linen is one of the most popular yarns on the American market because it is so well suited to all climatic conditions. Its appearance resembles slub cotton and it is usually mixed in blends of 55% linen, 45% cotton.

❖ ❖ ❖ ❖
Silk

Silk comes from the filament which is spun by the silk worm to make its cocoon. It is the most luxurious of natural fibres and has a 'live' quality which takes colour dyes to a deeper intensity than any other yarn. Wild or 'bourette' silk has a spongy texture which is unique in its appearance and handling properties.

❖ ❖ ❖ ❖
Wool and other animal fibres

Wool fibre comes from the fleece of sheep and has inherent warmth and resilience. It is the most versatile of fibres and can be spun and woven into the lightest crepes or the heaviest chunkies. Wool is ideal for the Irish weather. In its natural, untreated handspun state, it is almost 90% waterproof.

Another animal fibre is the luxurious long-haired mohair which comes from the angora goat, a breed which is more than 3000 years old ('angora' is derived from Ankara, the capital of Turkey). Mohair is one of the most popular fibres for handknitting because it is shiny, cool, crease-resistant and very expensive looking.

Other animal fibres include my own favourite, alpaca, which comes from the alpaca goat or South American llama. Alpaca is the most hard-wearing of all yarns. It has a unique thermal quality which makes it cool in the summer and warm in winter.

Finally there are cashmere (very soft goat hair) and angora (from the angora rabbit). Both are at the more expensive end of the range of animal fibres, but they are ideal for adding to a garment in small patches to create that very special effect.

❖ ❖ ❖ ❖
Thickness (or yarn 'count')

There are basically three counts of yarn which are the most popular with handknitters - Double knit (DK), Aran weight and chunky (mohair can be classed either as Aran or chunky). A very basic help in choosing the needles to suit the yarn (provided tension is fairly basic and standard) is to use the following formula as a rough guide.

Double knitting yarns - 3mm for ribs (or $3^1/_4$mm) and 4mm for body

Aran thickness (and some mohairs) - 4mm for ribs and 5mm (or $4^1/_2$ mm) for body

Chunky (and some mohairs) - 5mm for ribs and 6mm for body

Helpful Hints

- Remember that hairy yarns should be knitted quite loosely to avoid matting when washed. With mohair, it depends on how hairy the yarn is and how tight you would like the stitch structure to be.

- Hairy yarns must always be 'teased' or brushed sideways (against the grain of the knitting) after washing to separate fibres. All long-haired yarns go slightly 'into shock' when washed.

- Aran is usually the best wool to choose for beginners' knitting because it is knit on big needles, produces large stitches which are easy to follow, and gives a good unisex weight to the finished garment, which is extremely practical.

❖ ❖ ❖ ❖
2. CHOOSING THE RIGHT COLOURS

If you are at all worried about choosing colours which work well together, then stick to any of the following four groupings. The colours in these categories will mix well with each other, creating a beautiful tonal effect which will look very professional indeed.

Tonal groupings are the key (see colour plates). Keep the hot colours and the cold colours in separate statements, with the neutrals and pastels out on their own.

- *Neutrals* : coffee, mink, ivory or winter white (called Aran in Ireland), magnolia, brown, mixed with light and dark greys.
- *Naturals* : moss green, egg yellow, nettle green, rust, slate blue, indigo, lavender, purple, cochineal pink.
- *Hot colours* : red, orange, pink, yellow, salmon, cherry, chestnut.
- *Cool colours* : navy blue, royal blue, turquoise, jade, kelly green, lime, sky blue, aquamarine.

Helpful Hints

- Always remember that white and black are not colours and do not belong to any of these categories. They are tones which stand out totally on their own and which can therefore be slotted in to work with every colour under the sun.
- For ideas on colour groupings, ask your local artists' supplier for a paint colour chart. This will open up endless possibilities and variations. Designers use this technique all the time!

❖ ❖ ❖ ❖

3. A WELL-STOCKED WORKBOX

A knitter's well-stocked workbox should contain the following basic equipment:

> knitting needles
>
> measuring tape
>
> scissors
>
> needle gauge
>
> blunt-edged darning needles
>
> rustless steel pins
>
> stitch holders (to hold stitches not being worked)
>
> knitting register (for counting rows accurately). This is clipped onto the end of a needle.
>
> polythene bag (to keep work clean)
>
> a selection of wooden clothes pegs (to use as yarn holders if you intend to knit your design into the garment as you go along) or yarn holders

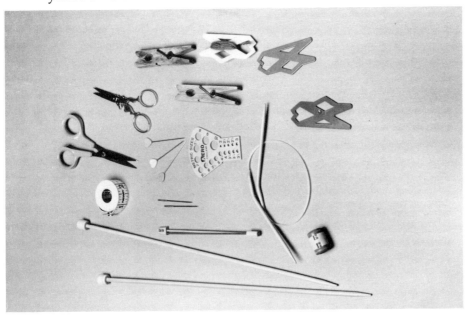

❖ ❖ ❖ ❖
Knitting Needles

Knitting needles can be purchased in steel, wood, bone and plastic, as well as a combination of steel and plastic. The ideal needle is lightweight and smooth, with points which taper gradually and which are not too sharp. Knitting needles come in different lengths. Always choose a length which will comfortably hold the stitches which are required for each design you create.

KNITTING NEEDLE CONVERSION CHART		
Metric	English	American
2mm	14	0
2¼mm	13	1
2¾mm	12	2
3mm	11	
3¼mm	10	3
3¾mm	9	5
4mm	8	6
4½mm	7	7
5mm	6	8
5½mm	5	9
6mm	4	10
6½mm	3	10½
7mm	2	
7½mm	1	
8mm	0	11
9mm	00	13
10mm	000	15

▲

Needle chart

Helpful Hints

- You should always discard a needle which has become the slightest bit rough as it will pull the wool and fluff it.

- Circular needles are marvellous for knitting garments 'all in one piece' to the armholes. They minimise the number of seams to be sewn up later.

- Bamboo needles are ideal for knitters who suffer from arthritis. These needles are lightweight and easier to work than standard needles.

❖ ❖ ❖ ❖
4. ESSENTIAL TECHNIQUES

❖ ❖ ❖ ❖
Threading up hands

Before starting to knit any garment, the hands must be threaded up correctly (see illustrations).

For a right-handed person, the yarn is looped around the fingers of the right hand to achieve even knitting. The needle which is used to create the stitches is held in the right hand. The left hand holds the needle with the made stitches ready for working.

A left-handed person will reverse the positions completely. It will make no difference at all to the finished garment.

The illustrations show just how easy threading up is for both right-handed and left-handed knitters. If you are teaching a left-handed person to knit, have them sit opposite you and do exactly as you do - as if you were creating a mirror image. If a left-handed person wants to follow a diagram in a book, simply place the illustration in front of a mirror and follow the instructions in reverse.

Helpful Hints

- You may find that your knitting tension is a little tight when you use this method of wrapping the yarn around your little finger. If this happens, just let the yarn slide through you last finger (as I do), catching it gently to achieve an even flow.

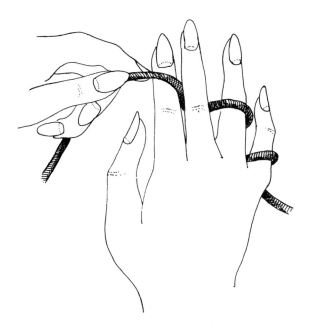

▲

Threading up hands: Right-handed method

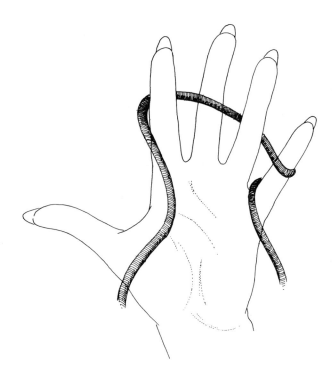

▲

Threading up hands: Left-handed method

❖ ❖ ❖ ❖
Casting on Stitches

(using the old Aran Island method)

This ancient method of casting on was first developed in the knitting schools of the Aran Islands. It was handed down from generation to generation because it produced a very firm 'double rope twist' edge on the base of each garment. It stood up to a tremendous amount of wear and tear and was of course suitable for all weather conditions.

The illustrations show how to cast on stitches in six basic steps.

❖ ❖ ❖ ❖
Instructions for Casting On

Make a loop in the end of the ball of yarn. Put this loop on the left-hand needle (1).

Holding the yarn in the right hand (left handers reverse the process), insert the right-hand needle into the loop (2). Wind the yarn under and over the point of the needle and draw a new loop through the first loop (3). Pass the newly-made loop onto the left-hand needle beside the first loop (4).

Now for the important part! Place the point of the right-hand needle *in between* the two loops on the left-hand needle (5). Wind the yarn under and over the point of the needle again and draw it through the new loop. Pass the newly-made loop onto the left-hand needle (6).

Continue in this way until the required number of stitches has been cast on.

Helpful Hint

- To achieve an even firmer edge on your knitting before beginning the ribs, work one row of twisted knit stitches into the *back* of each knit stitch. This will leave a decorative 'purl' double edge at the base of your knitting.

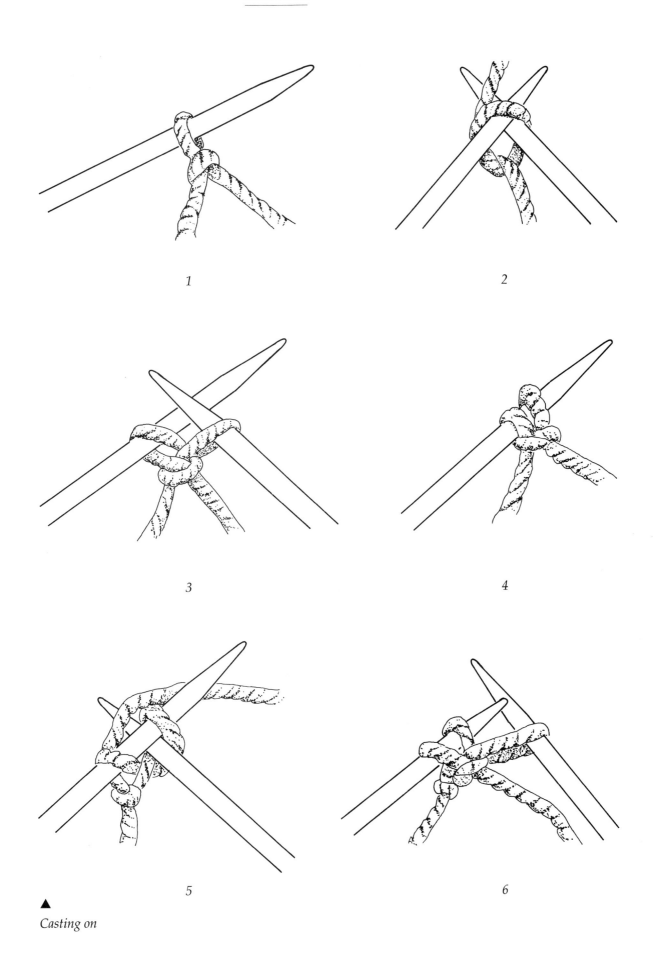

1

2

3

4

5

6

▲

Casting on

❖ ❖ ❖ ❖
5. BASIC STITCHES

❖ ❖ ❖ ❖
The Knit Stitch

The two stitches which must be perfected by any knitter are the *knit stitch* and the *purl stitch*.

To create the knit stitch (see photographs), hold the needle with the cast on stitches in the left hand. Hold the yarn and the other needle in the right hand.

Insert the point of the right-hand needle through the first stitch on the left-hand needle from the *front to the back*. Keeping the yarn at the *back* of the work, pass it under and over the top of the right-hand needle. Draw this loop through the stitch on the left-hand needle.

Keep the newly-made stitch on the right-hand needle and allow the stitch on the left-hand needle to slip off.

Repeat this action into each stitch on the left-hand needle until all stitches are transferred to the right-hand needle. You have now completed a row using the 'knit' stitch.

To work the next row, change the needle holding the stitches to the left hand so that the yarn is again in position at the beginning of the row. Hold the yarn and the free needle in your right hand.

▲
Knit Stitch. Step 1

▲
Knit Stitch. Step 2

▲
Knit Stitch. Step 3

Knit Stitch. Step 4

❖ ❖ ❖
The Garter Stitch

This is sometimes referred to as 'plain knitting'. It simply means that you knit every single row and is therefore an excellent stitch for anyone beginning knitting. The garter stitch results in a series of ridges (see photograph). It creates a rather heavy fabric with a horizontal elasticity to it.

▲

Garter Stitch

❖ ❖ ❖ ❖
The Purl Stitch

The photographs show clearly how to execute the second basic knitting stitch, the purl stitch.

Hold the needle with the cast on stitches in the left hand. Hold the yarn and the other needle in the right hand.

Insert the point of the right-hand needle through the 1st stitch on the left-hand needle from right to left. Keeping the yarn at the *front* of the work, pass it over and around the top of the right-hand needle. Draw this loop through the stitch on the left-hand needle.

Keep this newly-made stitch on the right-hand needle and allow the stitch on the left-hand needle to slip off.

Repeat this action into each stitch on the left-hand needle until all the stitches are transferred to the right-hand needle. You have now 'purled' one row.

To work the next row, change the needle holding the stitches to the left hand so that the yarn is again in position at the beginning of the row. Hold the yarn and free needle in the right hand.

▲
Purl Stitch. Step 1

▲
Purl Stitch. Step 2

▲
Purl Stitch. Step 3

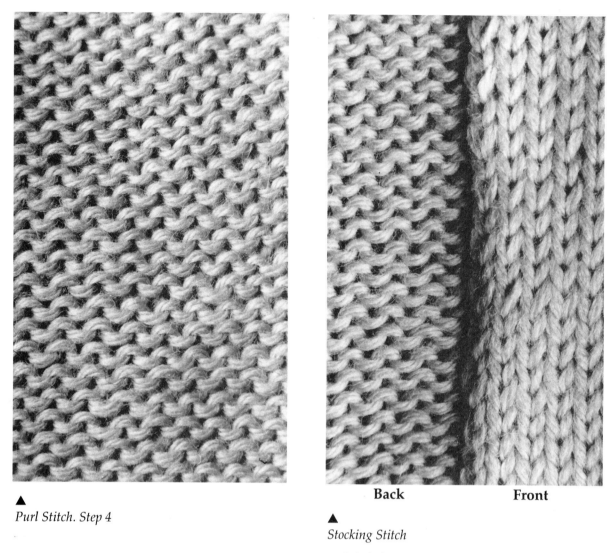

Purl Stitch. Step 4

Back   **Front**

Stocking Stitch

❖ ❖ ❖ ❖
The Stocking Stitch

This is sometimes called the 'stocking web' or 'plain smooth fabric'. It consists of alternate rows of knit stitches and purl stitches, thus bringing all the ridges to one side of the fabric (see photograph). The ridged side is usually regarded as the 'wrong' side of the work, but this can still be used to great effect as the 'right' side of the work. It is useful in showing up a pattern as it forms a very good background for Aran textural knitting stitches.

Helpful Hint

- The stocking stitch is the most commonly used knitting stitch. It is useful to remember that it was originally popular because it is more economical than any other stitch in both the time it takes to work and in the amount of material used.

❖ ❖ ❖ ❖
Picking up dropped stitches

There is a very simple way of picking up any dropped stitches, as the illustration shows.

Make sure you have the smooth side of your garment facing you. Then insert a crochet hook through the dropped stitch from the front and draw the loose strand from the row above through the loop. Repeat this process until the dropped stitch is back on the needle.

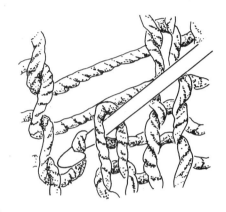

▲
Dropped Stitches: Picking up dropped stitches

Helpful Hint

● When you find a dropped stitch in your knitting, 'capture' it immediately by securing it to the row below with a small safety pin. If you don't, it will continue to unravel. Once secured with the pin, pick it up properly at the first possible moment.

❖ ❖ ❖ ❖
Counting Rows and Stitches

When you are working with a large number of stitches which form a pattern, it is a good idea to use a long coloured thread, knitted in with every 10th stitch, to make counting easier. This technique also works in counting rows by knitting the coloured thread in with the first stitch in every 10th row and looping the strands very loosely along the side.

This is an old Aran method which was used before row counters were invented. Today, a wide selection of stitch and row markers is available in most wool shops.

❖ ❖ ❖ ❖

6. RIB STITCH STRUCTURES

❖ ❖ ❖ ❖
Single Rib: Twisted Aran Method

This is one of the most useful of all knitting stitches as it forms an elastic fabric which always springs back into shape (see photograph). It can be used at the bottom of all knitted garments, as well as on the cuffs and at the neck. It is formed by knitting one stitch and purling the next and taking the yarn back and forth between the two stitches.

Single rib:
twisted Aran method

One very important point to bear in mind is that the old Aran 'twisted' ribs were always firmer than the straightforward method. This rib is formed by knitting into the *back* of the first stitch on the first row, bringing the yarn forward to the front of the work between the two needles. Purl the next stitch, then take the yarn back between the two needles, ready to knit into the back of the next stitch again. Continue in this way until all the stitches are transferred to the right-hand needle. On the next row, all the stitches that were *knitted* on the first row must be *purled*, and all the stitches that were purled must be knitted as in row 1. It is essential to remember that the yarn must be brought forward after knitting a stitch so that it is in the correct position, ready to purl the next stitch, and taken back again after purling a stitch so that it is in the correct position, ready to knit the next stitch.

Helpful Hint

- This method of knitting into the *back* of the knit stitch (instead of into the front, which is the usual method) tightens the rib as it twists the knit stitch. But it should only be used on ribs and not on a stocking stitch surface.

❖ ❖ ❖ ❖
Double Rib: Twisted Aran Method

A ribbed stitch structure consists of a combination of knit and purl stitches which form vertical lines. This has the effect of contracting the width of the work while still keeping the basic size. At the same time, it also makes the fabric very elastic. The amount of contraction produced depends largely upon the proportion of the knit-to-purl stitches. When the rib consists of an even number of knit and purl stitches, the contraction is greater and will be reduced as the difference becomes wider.

The double rib (or 2 x 2 rib, see photograph) is formed by knitting the first two stitches, then purling the second two stitches, and continuing on in this pattern to the end of the row. On the second row, knit where the knit stitches appear in front of you and purl where the purl stitches appear. You will gradually see that the thicker vertical lines of the knit ridges begin to dominate the surface.

Double rib:
twisted Aran method

Helpful Hint
- Always knit into the *back* of every knit stitch on this rib structure to keep it 'twisted' firmly into shape.

❖ ❖ ❖ ❖
'Moss Stitch' or Broken Rib Stitch Structure

This is a reversible stitch showing simple knit (K) and purl (P) stitches, alternating horizontally and vertically (see photograph). It is most easily worked on an uneven number of stitches by working every row K1, P1 to end, finishing with K1. If it has to be worked on an even number of stitches, the first row will begin K1, P1 and the second row P1, K1 etc.

Cast on a number of stitches which are divisible by 2, plus 1.

> 1st row - Knit 1, * purl 1, knit 1. Repeat from * to end.
>
> 2nd row - K 1, * P 1, K 1. Repeat from * to end.
>
> 3rd row - K 1, * P 1, K 1. Repeat from * to end.
>
> 4th row as 3rd

These four rows form the pattern.

Moss stitch

Helpful Hint

- When completed, this rib is very decorative in itself, but does not pull a garment in at the end. It is best suited to cotton, linen or silk. It forms a flat but firm rib.

❖ ❖ ❖ ❖
Irish Moss Stitch

This is a variation on the original moss stitch formula.

Cast on a number of stitches, divisible by 2, plus 1.

      1st row - K1, * P1, K1. Repeat from * to end.

      2nd row - P1, * K1, P1. Repeat from * to end.

      3rd row - as 2nd.

      4th row - as 1st.

These four rows form the pattern (see photograph).

Irish moss stitch

Helpful Hints

- This rib structure will not pull the garment in at the end. It ensures a fancy, firm edging and is most suitable for shorter style shapes.
- Try this stitch on both the button and buttonhole bands of a cardigan or jacket, while leaving the other ribs as pattern. It gives a much better surface for buttonholes and stops the bands from 'turning in'.

❖ ❖ ❖ ❖
Chequerboard Rib

This consists of blocks of stocking stitch and reversed stocking stitch. The pattern is worked over a multiple of 10 stitches plus 5.

Row 1: *K5, P5, * K5
  2: *P5, K5, * P5
  3: As Row 1
  4: * K5, P5, * K5 (this alternates the blocks)
  5: * P5, K5, * P5
  6: as Row 4

These six rows form the pattern. The formula is repeated from * to* on each row, then finishes with the last 5 sts after the second *.

▲
Chequerboard rib

❖ ❖ ❖ ❖
Wheatear Ribbing

This is a more decorative rib and adds a very special finish to any garment, as the photograph shows.

Cast on a number of stitches divisible by 5, plus 2.

1st row -   * P3. Put the needle behind the 1st stitch and K into the back of the 2nd st. Then K the 1st st and slip both sts off the needle together. Repeat from * to last 2 sts. P2.

2nd row -   * K2. P the 4th st, then the 3rd st, and slip both sts off the needle together. Repeat from * to last 3 sts. K3.

These two rows form the pattern.

Wheatear rib

Helpful Hint

- When you are working this fancy Aran twisted rib, you will notice that it 'pulls' the garment firmly in at the bottom. It is therefore one of the most suitable ribs for yarns such as cotton, linen or silk.

▲ *'Neutral' colours - coffees, minks, magnolias.*

▲ *Colours like moss green, egg yellow and nettle green are all 'naturals'*

▲ *Keep the colours 'hot' with shades including red, orange and pink.*

▲ *'Cool' colours comprise shades such as navy and royal blue, lime and turquoise.*

▲ *Basic crew neck sweater (page 74) modelled by Sylvia Myers.*
(Co-ordinates by Feathers, Malahide, Co. Dublin)

▲ *Actress and model Olivia Tracy wears 'Bold Flowers' sweater dress (page 76).*

▲ *Jacqui Burke, lead singer in the Galway band Speakeasy, wears the 'Navajo Indian Ethnic Waistcoat' (page 78).*
(Co-ordinates by Mitsu, Malahide, Co. Dublin)

▲ *Actor Graham Wilkinson models the 'Acoustic Guitar Waistcoat' (page 80).*

❖ ❖ ❖ ❖
Edwardian Rib

Cast on any number of stitches.

Row	1	(wrong side):	Knit
	2		Purl

Repeat the last 2 rows once more.

Row	5	Purl
	6	K.
	7	P.
	8	K.
	9	P.
	10	K.

Repeat these 10 rows again and again to form the pattern.

▲

Edwardian rib

❖ ❖ ❖ ❖
Hems

A hem can add that special finish and weight to a coat or jacket. As a new trend, many sweater shapes have hems at the bottom instead of ribs because Swiss darning or Fairisle both work very well on this surface and can be so decorative.

❖ ❖ ❖ ❖
Stocking Stitch Hems

Cast on the required number of stitches for your garment. Starting with a knit (K) row, work approximately 2 inches of stocking stitch. End with a purl (P) row facing.

Now, instead of working this in a purl stitch, *knit* this one row (through the back of all stitches) so that it becomes a purl ridge on the right side of your garment. When you knit through the back of the loops in this way, it strengthens the folding edge and makes it more elastic.

Beginning with a knit row again, work exactly the same amount of rows again, *plus* one extra row to end with a purl row. Turn the hem to the wrong side after your garment is finished, and slip stitch into place. The purl ridge forms the fold line. (See photograph.)

▲
Sewn hem

▲
Knitted-in hem

Helpful Hints

- You will get a neater finish to a hem if you knit it together rather than slip stitching it. To make a 2 inch hem, knit as for stocking stitch hem, but stop 2 rows less after the fold line, again ending with a purl row. Pick up the stitches of the cast on row with a third needle and hold these behind the stitches that are already on the left-hand needle, with both points of the needles at the right hand. Knit to the end of the row, on the right side, working one stitch together from each needle (see photograph above).

- One way of ensuring that your hem remains firm and does not 'turn under' is always to knit the first stocking stitch section on needles that are $^1/_2$ mm smaller than the rest of the body. Change to the larger needles after the purl ridge turning row.

❖ ❖ ❖ ❖
Crochet Ribs

Crochet hooks are made of bone, steel or composition materials. When choosing a crochet hook, make sure that it is smooth and that it has a sharp point to go through the stitch easily. I use this simple personal guide when choosing my own hooks.

DK yarns - 3.5 to 4mm hook

Aran yarns - 4 to 4.5mm hook

Chunky (mohair) - 5.5 to 6mm hook

❖ ❖ ❖ ❖
Basic Stitches in Crochet

I find that crochet can be one of the easiest and most professional methods of finishing off necklines and front rib bands on knitted garments.

❖ ❖ ❖ ❖
Chain Stitch

Make a slip knot and place it on the hook. Now, holding the hook in the right hand with the thread between the thumb and first finger (held taut by the second and third fingers and looped under the little finger), pass the hook under the thread and pull the loop through. Continue in this way until a sufficient length of chain has been made.

When you are adding crochet ribs to knitting, you do not need a chain as your base edge because you will be using the cast off knitted edge. In the case of front cardigan bands, the raw knitted edge of your garment is used to work along sideways.

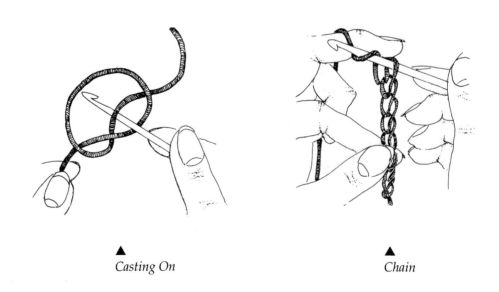

▲
Casting On

▲
Chain

❖ ❖ ❖ ❖
Double Crochet or 'Doubles'

Insert the hook into the foundation. Pass the hook under the thread and pull the loop through the row. Pass the hook under the thread again and draw the loop through both loops on the hook (see illustrations).

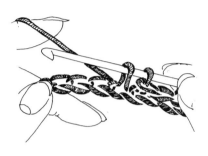

▲
Doubles A

▲
Doubles B

❖ ❖ ❖ ❖
Treble Crochet or 'Trebles'

Pass the hook under the thread and then into the foundation. Pass it under the thread again and draw a loop through. There are now three loops on the hook. Pass the hook under the thread and draw through the first two loops on the hook under the thread and then draw through the remaining loops (see illustration).

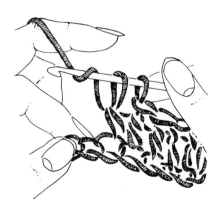

▲
Trebles

Helpful Hints

- Although there is a wide variety of crochet stitches, I find these three are always the best when working on a knitted surface. The marvellous thing about crochet is that it is three times easier than knitting and three times faster. You only have to worry about three stitches (at most) on the needle or hook at the one time.

- If any of the ribs at the bottom of your knitted garments have become loose, tighten them up by working three rows of crochet 'doubles' all around the cast-on edge. Hold your garment upside down and 'draw' the sample in to fit your requirements. Necks can also be tightened in this way. A crochet edge is firmer and stronger than a knitted one, and it is also more versatile.

- American crochet terminology is different from that used in Europe. If you are using American books, the following chart is a helpful reference.

European	American
1. chain	1. chain
2. single crochet	2. slip
3. double crochet	3. single crochet
4. half treble	4. half double
5. treble crochet	5. double crochet
6. double treble crochet	6. treble crochet
7. treble treble crochet	7. double treble crochet
8. quadruple treble crochet	8. long treble crochet
9. Tunisian crochet	9. Afghan stitch

❖ ❖ ❖ ❖
7. TENSION

Most knitters are inclined to brush the importance of tension aside. They don't bother to knit a tension square before attempting the finished garment. But creating the right tension can either make or break your knitting, so pay close attention to this section!

The term 'tension' means the number of stitches across and the number of rows down which are required to make one square inch of knitted fabric. Before you begin any garment, you must always knit a tension sample using the wool and needles specified in the pattern instructions. When you are designing something yourself, a tension sample 4 inches square is usually sufficient to enable you to measure the tension accurately. But if you are using a large, elaborate pattern, it is always worthwhile working a larger sample. *The importance of knitting this tension sample cannot be too heavily stressed!* Without it, you may either run short of wool, or you may have too much wool left over if you get the measurements wrong.

This formula of knitting a 4-inch square tension sample should only be used as a guide for plain stocking stitch fabric. Ribs and fancy patterns tend to 'draw in', thus producing more stitches to the inch. They may also spiral and produce fewer stitches to the inch.

❖ ❖ ❖ ❖
Width

Average knitters will find that their samples are correct. But if your stocking stitch is tighter (if you get more stitches to the inch) or looser (if you get fewer stitches to the inch), you must adjust by using larger needles in the first instance and smaller needles in the second.

❖ ❖ ❖ ❖
Length

It is very difficult to lay down strict and definite rules for the row tension, since this is apt to vary with the individual knitter. But it can be allowed for by using a measurement instead of counting rows.

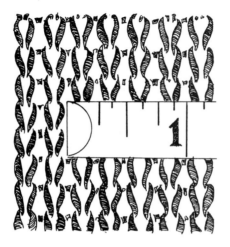

▲
Measuring the tension of stitches

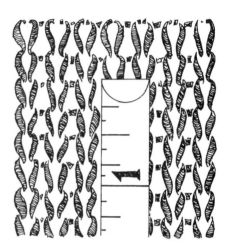

▲
Measuring the tension of rows

Helpful Hint

• When measuring tension, always take great care not to overlook half rows or half stitches. These will make an enormous difference over the whole width or length of the garment.

❖ ❖ ❖ ❖

8. THE BASIC DROP-SHOULDER SWEATER SHAPE

❖ ❖ ❖ ❖
Check List

- Choose the yarn and pattern. It is very important to go for a classic, comfortable shape when looking at designs. Don't be taken in by the design and colours shown, as these can be changed to suit your own needs.

- Check the needle sizes and decide on the colours that are available in the chosen yarn quality.

- Have a look at the rib structure of your pattern. Think about whether you will stick with a plain one or opt for a more fancy effect. Also check the length of the ribs at the bottom of the front and back and make sure you are happy with the size of the rib.

❖ ❖ ❖ ❖
Begin Knitting

1. Using correct smaller-sized needles for the rib, and with your chosen yarn, cast on stitches and work the required length of rib on the back of the garment.

2. Change to larger needle size after the rib, and work in plain stocking stitch to the armholes. It is this basic stitch which forms the main body of the garment. As there is no shaping at the armholes on this style of sweater, it is essential to use a piece of coloured thread tied onto each end of the row where you intend the armhole to begin. The armhole gap is usually 10 inches for women and 12 inches for men (as a rough guide). This part of the garment is where the sleeves will be sewn onto the main body.

3. After the armholes, the next part of any garment is the neckline. On the back of the sweater, it is very easy because this seam is usually without any shaping at all.

Knit the required armhole measurement and then simply cast off.

The front of the garment will require a dropped neckline which usually begins 2¹/₂ inches shorter than the back. This means that you complete your piece until it is measuring this much shorter than the back. Then put a number of centre stitches on a holder at the front neck opening and cast off stitches on the following rows at each side of the neck to gradually widen it until the sample is the same length as the back.

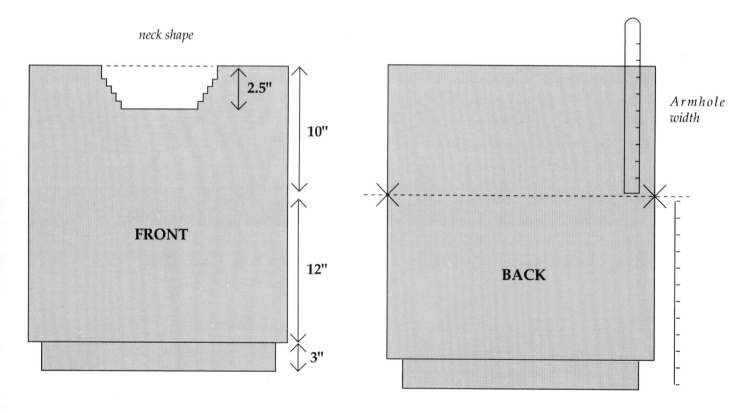

▲ *Basic drop-shoulder sweater shape*

❖ ❖ ❖ ❖
Casting off Stitches
(Back neckline of garment)

Always cast off in pattern. In the stocking stitch, this means that you cast off knitwise on a knit row and purlwise on a purl row. Casting off ribbing should always be done as if you were continuing in rib.

Knitwise (see photograph): Knit the first 2 sts from the left-hand needle to the right-hand needle. Using the left-hand needle, lift the first stitch on the right-hand needle over the second stitch. Then drop it off the needle. Knit the next stitch and repeat the procedure.

Casting off knitwise

Purlwise (see photograph): Purl the first 2 sts. Then, using the left-hand needle, lift the first stitch over the second and drop it off the needle. Purl the next stitch and repeat the procedure.

Casting off purlwise

❖ ❖ ❖ ❖
Increasing

The old name for increasing was 'widening', while decreasing was known as 'narrowing'. These terms still appear on some knitting patterns.

When you are shaping garments, the increasing should always be worked on the front of the fabric, and preferably not on the first or last stitch in a row, as this would cause an irregular seam when joined. The best method is to work on the third stitch from the beginning or end of the row.

There are several ways of increasing the number of stitches in a garment to produce the necessary shaping. The most popular is the 'invisible' method of knitting or purling twice into the same stitch, where you knit (or purl) into the front and back. The 'made' stitch is practically invisible and the appearance of the fabric remains undisturbed (see Method 1 in illustration).

The second method of increasing is by knitting or purling into a loop between the stitches of the *previous row*. If you pick up the loop with the needle and twist it by knitting into the back of it, this will close up the hole which would otherwise be made, and which would subsequently spoil the evenness of the work (see Method 2 in illustration).

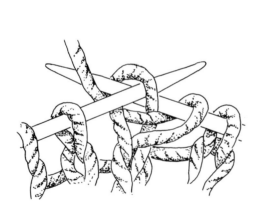

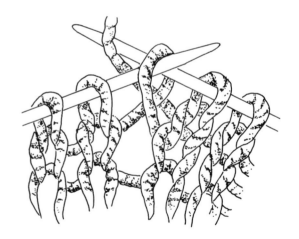

Increasing:
▲ *Method 1*   ▲ *Method 2*

Helpful Hint

● These two methods are best to use on sleeve shaping, 3 sts in on either side, because they do not interfere with the raw edge of the seam, thus making the sewing up easier.

❖ ❖ ❖
How to pick up stitches

Method 1 (see illustration)

On a horizontal part of your garment, you can pick up one stitch from every stitch on your knitting using a crochet hook.

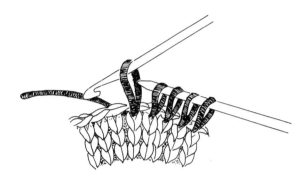

Method 2 (see illustration)

Pick up the front thread of your cast-off stitch using your knitting needle.

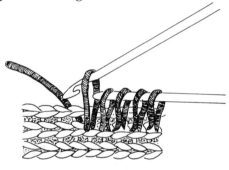

Method 3 (see illustration)

Another way of picking up the front thread of your cast-off stitch using your knitting needle.

❖ ❖ ❖ ❖
Decreasing Stitches

Neck Shaping (Front of Garment)

Decreasing should always be done over the first three or last three stitches. It should *never* be done at the raw edge as this will leave an awkward line when you go to pick up stitches for the neck rib. The professional way of shaping the neckline is to use the 'fully-fashioned' method. If you do not *show* your line of shaping, the garment may as well be a mass-produced 'cut and sew' sample. All the buyers in the designer stores on the export market look for this very professional finish. It is the 'handwriting' of a hand-knitted garment and gives it that more expensive finish (see photograph).

Formula

Decide where you need to decrease the stitches on your knitting. This is the point at which your fully-fashioned shaping should take place.

The method is to knit one stitch, slip the next stitch onto the needle without knitting it, knit the 3rd stitch, and then pass the slipped stitch *over* the 3rd stitch. (On commercial patterns, the abbreviation for this will appear as: K1, SL1, PSSO.) This method will form a line of shaping which slopes to the left.

When you want the line to slope to the right, knit along the row until you come to the last 3 stitches. Then knit 2 stitches together by putting the needle into the *front* of the 2nd stitch and taking off the first stitch behind it at the same time. Knit the last stitch. This way of shaping will slope evenly up both sides of the neck.

▲

Decreasing: Step 1

▲ *Decreasing: Step 2*

▲ *Decreasing: Step 3*

Helpful Hint

- Decreasing is *never* done on a purl row unless absolutely necessary because it can create an uneven look on the front of your knitting.

❖ ❖ ❖ ❖
Grafting Shoulders

This is a marvellous way of cutting down on sewing up a garment. It is a means by which you knit the two shoulder seams at the same time. They interlock, forming an invisible seam.

To graft stocking stitch fabric or knit edges together at the shoulder of a garment, transfer the stitches from the stitch holders onto the two needles, one behind the other, with the same number of stitches on each needle. Break the yarns, leaving an end three times the length of the edges to be grafted. Thread this around your right hand to 'knit' the stitches. Cast them off together to form a grafted invisible seam.

Important : Turn the work to the wrong side - that is, the purl side is facing you and the knitted sides are face-to-face in between the needles. The work will be turned to the right side (knit side) when the grafting is complete. Make sure the needle points are facing to the right.

Hold both needles in the left hand. Using a third needle, place the point of the needle in the right hand into the back of the 1st stitch on the front needle as if to knit it. Then, also slip the needle into the back of the 1st stitch on the back needle and draw the yarn under and over, pulling it through both stitches and knitting them as one stitch. This stitch is transferred to the right-hand needle and slipped off the left-hand one.

Repeat this until there are two stitches on the right-hand needle. Then slip the 1st stitch over the 2nd one, leaving only 1 stitch on a needle at a time. Cast off the stitches on the left-hand needle by knitting 2 stitches at a time. Every time you get 2 sts on the right-hand needle, slip the one on the right side over the left one so there is never more than one stitch on that needle at any one time.

Helpful Hint

- It is easier to knit into the back of the stitches, as knitting into the front of the two stitches at the same time is a bit difficult.

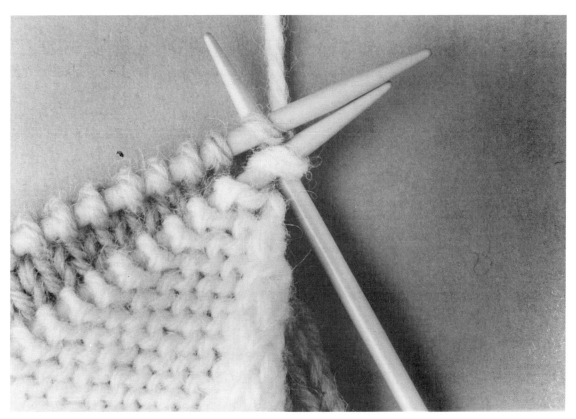

▲ *Step 1: Knitting the seam together using three needles*

▲ *Step 2: Casting off the stitches as you go along*

❖ ❖ ❖ ❖
9. BEFORE SEWING UP

❖ ❖ ❖ ❖
Blocking and Pressing

When working with natural fibres, it is always necessary to *block out* each piece to the correct size and shape.

When pressing, place each piece right side down on an ironing pad with three layers of cotton sheets underneath. This serves to 'cushion' the garment and to make sure it does not flatten too much. Pin it securely round the edges of the pad using rustless pins. Never stretch the knitting or the pins will tend to make an uneven edge. Take care to see that the stitches and rows run in straight lines. Using a measuring tape, check that the width and length are as you want them.

Place a clean, damp cloth over the item to be pressed. Then press the iron down on top of the cloth and lift it up again without moving it over the surface of the garment. Each area should be pressed evenly, but not too heavily, before lifting the iron to go on to the next area. Ribbing or garter stitch edges must *never* be pressed or they will loose their elasticity.

Note : Remember that all wools and yarns go slightly 'into shock' when they are being twisted and twined in the knitting process. They therefore need to be steamed a little to loosen and soften the fibres into shape. In this way, they will regain the initial softness which they had in their original ball or hank form. This is most important, as every machine knitter knows that knit pieces need to be steamed to get them to 'settle' into their correct shape — and there is really no difference in the hand-knitting process. This professional finishing technique is what gives a garment that very special designer quality, no matter how simple the shape or stitch structure. It ensures that it will 'hang' correctly on the wearer.

Helpful Hints

- In most knitwear factories, they have a 'steam press' to give the samples that professional feel after they are completely finished. Remember that most dry cleaners have one of these machines and will 'steam' your garment for anything up to £1 while you wait. This is particularly useful for Aran and chunky wool garments because it is very difficult to get them to sit properly by just using the home iron method.

- Never steam or press ribs. Be sure that your local dry cleaner also takes note of this!

❖ ❖ ❖ ❖
Sewing up Seams

The choice of seaming method will depend largely on the type of garment. But I find the invisible seaming method has always proved the best with any type of knitting. There are no hard edges if it is sewn up on the outside.

Use a blunt-ended darning needle and the original yarn for joining the pieces together. Remember, you are always working on the outside. So with the right side of both pieces facing, take the first loop from the first stitch on one side and the second loop from the first stitch on the other side and top stitch together (see illustration). Do this on every second row, if desired, as it is not always necessary to work it on every row, stitch for stitch. But be very careful not to 'pull' the seam. This means that you are taking a loop from the first stitch on each side and splicing them together to form one stitch. It may seem a little unusual when you start off the seam, as it will be quite visible. But because you are working along the grain of the garment, you will find that the seam begins to close over after you and that the stitching becomes completely invisible. This gives a perfect straight seam with a neat line on the inside of the garment.

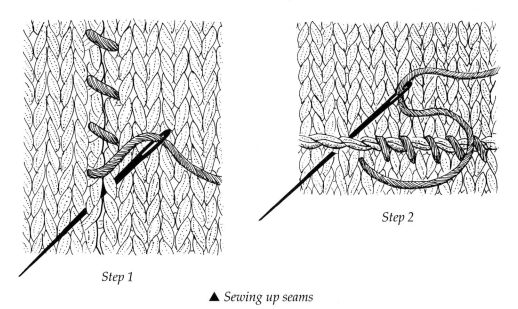

Step 1

Step 2

▲ *Sewing up seams*

❖ ❖ ❖ ❖
10. LOOKING AFTER YOUR KNITWEAR

❖ ❖ ❖ ❖
Care in Washing

The correct aftercare of all knitted garments is just as important as the knitting itself. First, check the ball band on all yarns for instructions. If you are in any doubt, always hand wash. It is essential that the minimum amount of handling occurs when the fabric is wet. *Before washing, always turn the garment inside out.* Never lift the item by the shoulders. Squeeze out any excess moisture very gently, but never wring the garment.

I always find it good to suggest to people that they treat the garment as they would treat their own hair. Use gentle soap flakes and fabric conditioner to keep the yarn from hardening. Use baby shampoo for those very special fibres such as mohair, alpaca or angora. Always rinse two or three times to make sure that all soap deposits have been thoroughly removed.

Once the garment has been rinsed, gently lift it out onto the draining board, supporting the weight with both hands. Then prepare the drying area.

First, place three or four old newspapers over the surface which will be used for drying. Spread out the papers well beyond the size of the garment. Cover the papers with two clean towels which are colour fast.

Gently lift the garment onto the centre of the towels. Spread it to its original shape and place it flat gently on the towel, smoothing out all the creases. Leave the garment until all the excess moisture has been absorbed by the towels and newspapers. Then - and only then - should it be carefully lifted and placed on the clothes line for the final airing.

❖ ❖ ❖ ❖
Aftercare

No matter how careful you are, knitting can become snagged, or the yarn may 'pile' into little balls of fluff. It is very easy to sort out these problems.

To prevent snagging, never wear jewellery which will catch in the yarn. If you discover a snag, never cut it off or the garment will unravel. Use a blunt needle and push the snagged end through to the wrong side of the fabric. Gently tighten the yarn until the stitch is the correct size. Then knot the end of yarn and leave it on the inside of the garment.

When piling occurs, gently pull off the balls of yarn with a clothes brush or a teasel.

Helpful Hints

- Rather than pegging the garment to the line, which can distort the shape, take a pair of old tights or panty hose and put a leg through each arm, with the gusset of the tights supporting the neck area. Pin the toes and gusset of the tights to the line instead of the garment. This supports the knitting along the full weight of the sleeves, shoulders and neckline. It also allows the air to rush through the garment to soften and loosen the fibres.

- The handle of a sweeping brush slid through one sleeve and out the other is another great way of drying a garment. Get two clothes hangers and hang them on your clothes line. Then balance the brush handle between them.

- Never hang your knitwear out in the open as the sun's rays will alter the colour. If you must put your garment outdoors, make sure you put a sheet over the whole garment.

- Most yarn shops now have very good little combs to help you deal with the problem of piling. They are called 'De Fuzz It' or 'Fuzz Off' and will fit neatly into any small handbag. A must for anyone who values their knitwear!

- There is a new protein shampoo to care for knitwear on the market. It is phosphate free, includes a deodorising agent to provide lasting freshness, and gives a luxury finish to all fabrics. It is called 'Angora Washcream' and contains 40-50 handwashes.

11. FINISHING TOUCHES

❖ ❖ ❖ ❖
Buttonholes

Buttonhole bands will be needed for all types of cardigans, jackets and coats, as well as for all those shirt-style sweaters with front neck openings. These buttonholes are usually worked on a separate border. This means that you will have a plain ribbed band on one side of the cardigan, which is knitted separately on smaller needles than the main body, and sewn on afterwards. The button will be attached to this side. On the opposite band, it will be necessary to decide on the gap between each hole and then knit the band until the buttonhole position is reached, ending at the centre front edge. On the next row, work a few stitches until the position of the buttonhole is reached. Cast off the required number of stitches for the buttonhole (usually 1 for a cardigan, 2 for a jacket or coat) and pattern to the end of the row. On the next row, cast on the number of stitches (over the gap) to complete the buttonhole.

Repeat this action for as many buttonholes as required. All buttonholes need to be neatened and reinforced when they are finished. This can be done by working around them in a buttonhole stitch using the same yarn. (See also Embroidery chapter.)

❖ ❖ ❖ ❖
Buttonhole Stitch

Work along both sides of the opening in the buttonhole stitch for a horizontal buttonhole opening, neatening each end with 3 straight stitches. Take care not to work too many stitches around the opening so the edges become stretched. On the other hand, too few stitches would tighten the opening.

Helpful Hint

- To avoid spoiling the buttonhole by a loose loop of yarn at one end - the result of casting on the same number of stitches - work to the stitch *before* the cast-off stitches and increase in *this* stitch by working into the front and back of it. Then cast on one stitch less than was cast off in the previous row.

Buttonholes

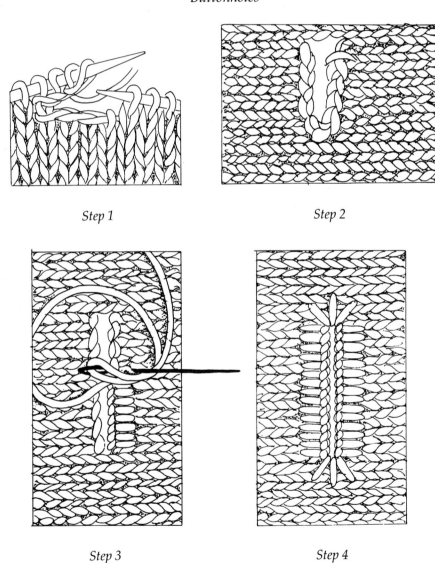

Step 1

Step 2

Step 3

Step 4

❖ ❖ ❖ ❖
Covered Buttons

Buttons which do not exactly match the colour of your yarn can spoil the whole appearance of a garment. The cheap and simple answer is to make knitted buttons to cover button moulds or old buttons. Always use fine needles to keep the fabric tight.

Basic formula

With 3mm needles and using Aran weight wool, cast on 4 stitches. Work every row in a stocking stitch (knit 1 row, purl 1 row), increase in every row at each end until 12 stitches are on the needle. Then work 4 or 6 rows straight (depending on the size of your buttonhole). Decrease at each end of every row after that until only 4 stitches remain. Cast off.

Gather over wooden mould (or old button).

You can work many variations of this button in smaller or larger sizes once you know the basic formula. If you are working in double knitting yarn, use 2mm needles for buttons. Use 4mm needles when working in mohair or chunky. The key is that you use one full size smaller than the needles you choose for the rib on your main pattern.

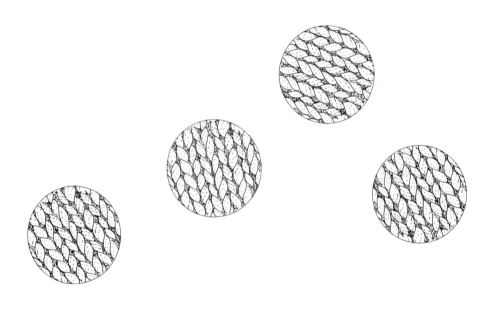

▲ *Covered buttons*

Helpful Hint

- Collect old buttons for covering rather than buying moulds. Once you select the same size button for each garment, they need not necessarily be the same colour as you will be covering them anyway.

❖ ❖ ❖ ❖
Knit Shoulder Pads

Basic formula

With 5mm needles and Aran weight yarn, cast on 38 stitches. Work 40 rows in a knit 1, purl 1 rib. Cast off. Fold the square into the shape of a triangle and sew down. Set the top of the triangle at the neck shoulder edge. Place the wide base along the shoulder part of the sleeve seam.

For drop-shoulder sweaters, set the top of the triangle at the neck shoulder. Slip stitch the wide base half-way across the shoulder seam on the inside of the garment.

Knit Shoulder Pads

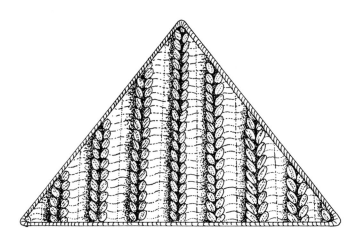

▲ *Knit shoulder pad*

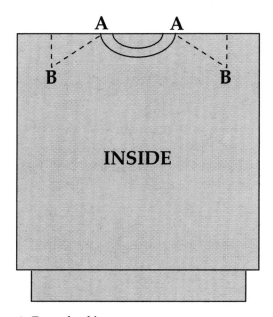

▲ *Drop-shoulder sweater*

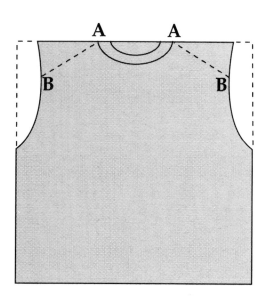

▲ *Set-in sleeve style*

❖ ❖ ❖ ❖
Pockets

Inset pockets are usually more practical for knitted garments than patch pockets. They also look much more professional. Sometimes, of course, it is easier to have patch pockets because they can be made separately and sewn into position when the garment is finished. In this case, the invisible method of 'sewing up on the outside' is very important.

To make a straight inset pocket (see illustration), knit the lining of the pocket to the width and depth required and leave on a spare needle. When the position of the pocket is reached in knitting the garment, cast off the same number of stitches as the pocket lining. On the following row, work across the stitches of the lining in place of the cast-off stitches.

To complete the pocket, the border may be either knitted separately and sewn on afterwards to the cast-off edge, or the cast-off stitches may be picked up and knitted up for the depth required. A third method is to make the border in one with the pocket by leaving the stitches for the pocket top on a stitch holder instead of casting them off and then knitting them on for the border. If you prefer your pocket to have no border, a row or two of double crochet will neaten it.

When sewing pocket linings into position, see that the edges follow a straight line of stitches.

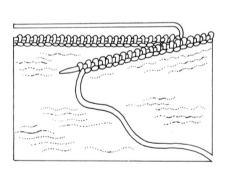

▲

The lining stitches cast on for a vertical pocket

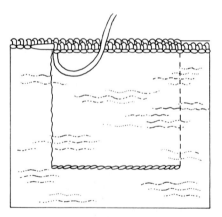

▲

When the lining is the required depth, the stitches are worked together with the main work stitches.

❖ ❖ ❖ ❖
Knitting Appliqué Sheep

These sheep are fantastic for kids' sweaters or for giving adults' sweaters that 'country look'.

You will need some cream or white bouclé yarn. This is like slub yarn, the 'thick and thin' variety. If you don't have bouclé yarn, chunky Aran will do. If the yarn which you have available is too thin, simply double it.

Using a pair of 6mm needles, cast on 6 stitches (or 4, or 8, or 10 - depending on the size you want). Knit a square in garter stitch - all knit rows. Cast off. Sew the square onto the garment, which should be in stocking stitch.

Using a black double knit strand of wool (grey or brown will also do nicely) and chain stitch embroidery, work the face, feet and tail. The ears are made up of two loops which are fastened down separately. The centre of the face is filled in with loops.

Don't be disappointed if your initial efforts end up looking like a 'mouse on stilts'. Practice makes perfect!

▲ *Knitted appliqué sheep*

❖ ❖ ❖ ❖

12. DESIGNER DETAILS

The difference between an expensive designer knit and an ordinary 'home knit' is found in the attention to detail, both in the finishing method as well as the special touches which personalise the garment.

Helpful Hints

- Add hand-knit covered buttons to all your own knitwear.
- Always put knitted triangular shoulder pads into your garments, whether they have drop shoulders or shaped set-in sleeves. This stops the weight of the sleeve from dragging the shoulder seam down.
- Apply a little creative embroidery, Swiss darning or hand painting to your finished article.
- Sew your own personalised labels into your knitwear. These can be ordered in small quantities from your local wool store.
- Embroider your initials into the corner of each garment. American buyers in the big department stores often insist on each designer 'signing' his or her creation.

❖ ❖ ❖ ❖

13. EMBROIDERY

Embroidery can easily be worked *over* knitting without the need of charts or graphs. (The only type of applied embroidery which requires a chart is Swiss darning.) Simple embroidery stitches such as a chain stitch or a stem stitch can be used to show up a seam, create a vertical stripe or highlight certain details in a Swiss darned design. The ideas are endless and very effective.

When planning a design, try something very simple and geometric at first. You can proceed to more difficult designs as you gain confidence. The stitches demonstrated in this book can be incorporated in a wide variety of ways. All of them can be easily worked on a plain stocking stitch background.

Helpful Hint

- Care must be taken when working out the exact position for each embroidery stitch. I find that artists' Conté chalk (brick red in colour) is best for this purpose. It holds its colour a little better than tailors' chalk, or other chalks, on the uneven surface. It usually comes in an oblong stick or pencil and can be purchased from any artists' materials shop. It does not stain the garment and can be easily rubbed away afterwards. *Never* use oil pastels on a knitted fabric as they will be impossible to remove.

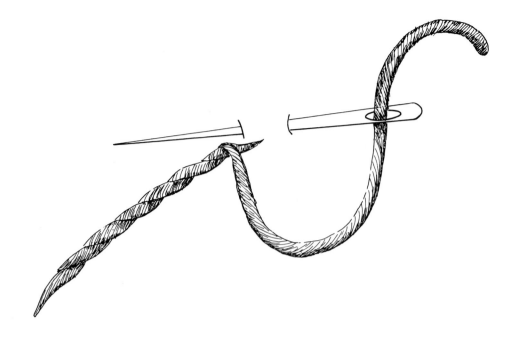

▲ *Stem Stitch*

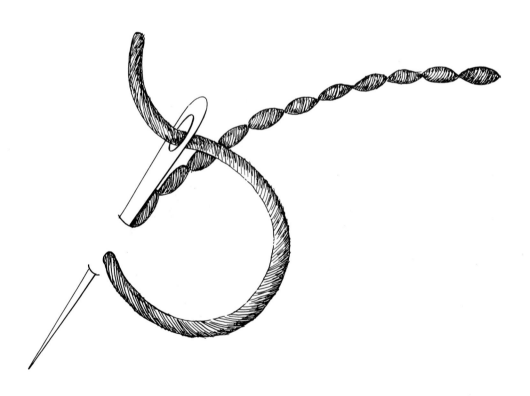

▲ *Back Stitch*

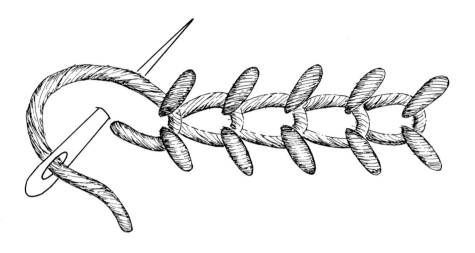

▲ *Wheatear Stitch*

▲ *Spider's Web*

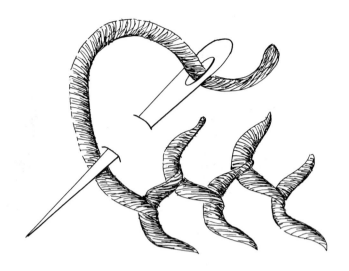

▲ *Feather Stitch*

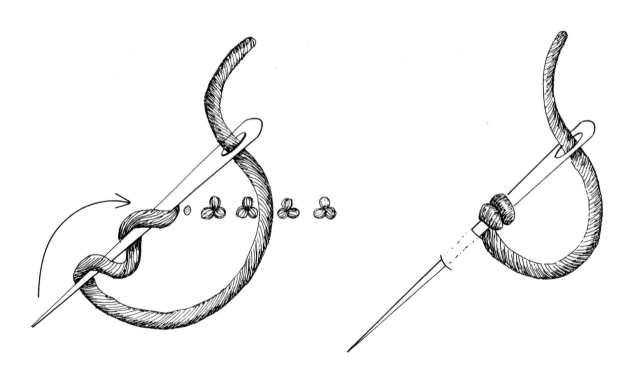

▲ *French Knot*

▲ *Chain Stitch*

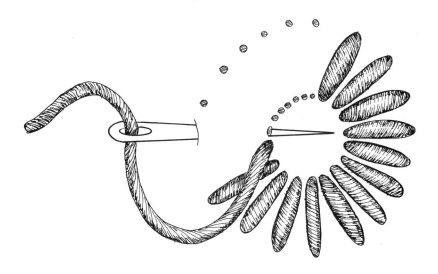

▲ *Straight Stitch*

▲ *Split Stitch*

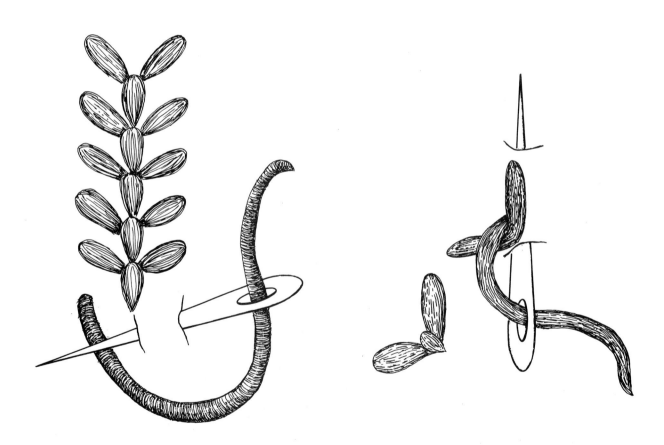

▲ *Fly Stitch*

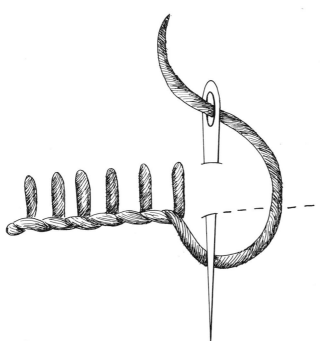

▲ *Buttonhole Stitch*

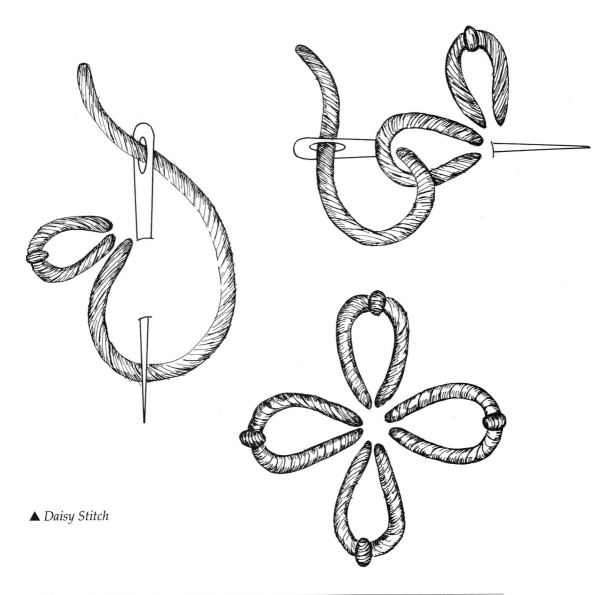

▲ *Daisy Stitch*

▲ *Stem and Chain Stitch Design*

▲ *Stem, Chain and Daisy Design*

❖ ❖ ❖ ❖
14. SWISS DARNING EMBROIDERY

Swiss darning embroidery is a very old method used to replace Fairisle. It is a quick and simple way of applying designs to finished garments. The stitch looks exactly like Fairisle. It is worked row by row and stitch by stitch from a graph chart. The difference between 'creative' embroidery and Swiss darning is that the former sits *on top* of the knitted fabric, while Swiss darning becomes part of the surface itself and blends down into the knitted stitches.

❖ ❖ ❖ ❖
Creating your own designs

To design your own Swiss darning motifs, why not start by selecting a picture from a magazine or children's book? Make sure the image is very simple in both shape and design.

1. Outline the picture by placing tracing paper over it. Use sellotape to secure the tracing paper. Copy the outline onto the tracing paper using a HB pencil.

2. Remove the tracing paper and turn it back to front. Using a 6B (very soft) pencil, blacken the back of the design.

3. Place a sheet of graph paper behind the tracing paper and secure it with sellotape. The blackened area should be facing the graph paper. Go over the front of the design again, using the HB pencil, by leaning gently down on the outline so that it will show up clearly on the graph paper.

4. Remove the tracing paper. You should be able to see the pencil outline of your design on the graph paper. Square out the outline, like a computer drawing. Every square now represents a stitch.

5. Using colouring pencils (*not* markers or paint!) fill in the various shapes on your design so that they are very clear to the eye.

6. Outline the design onto your knitwear with Swiss darning, filling in the colours as you go along.

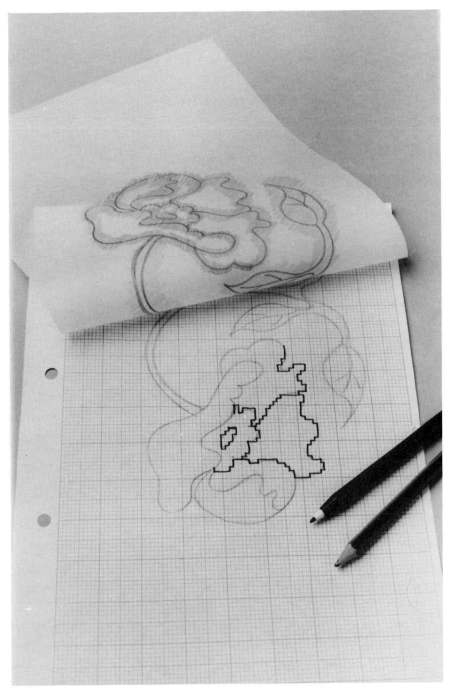

▲ *Transferring design onto graph paper*

Helpful Hint

- It is useful to note that double knitting (DK) fabric should be Swiss darned with DK yarn. Aran-weight fabric should also be Swiss darned with DK, and chunky with Aran weight.

❖ ❖ ❖ ❖
Swiss Darning Technique

Work only on a stocking stitch base. Use a large darning needle and a weight of yarn which is appropriate to the garment (see 'Helpful Hint' page 65). Begin at the bottom right of the motif.

Photograph 1

Working from the back, bring up the needle to the right side of the work, through the stitch *below* the first stitch to be worked.

Photograph 2

Insert the needle around the back of the stitch just *above* the one to be covered.

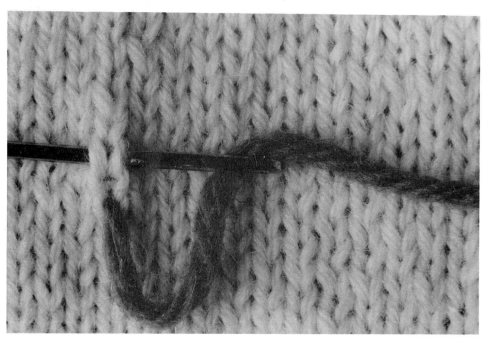

▲ *Model Catherine O'Keeffe wears the 'Wild Flower Waistcoat' (page 82).*
(Co-ordinates by Mitsu, Malahide, Co. Dublin)

▲ *Graham Wilkinson with the 'Piano Waistcoat' (page 84).*

▲ *Olivia Tracy models the 'Peblum Tapestry Jacket' (page 86).*
(Co-ordinates by Feathers, Malahide, Co. Dublin)

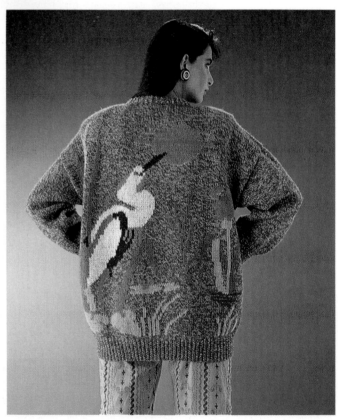

▲ *Front and back of the 'Wild Heron Jacket' modelled by Sylvia Myers (page 88).*
(Co-ordinates by Mitsu, Malahide, Co. Dublin)

Photograph 3

Now insert the needle back into the stitch below, where it first emerged, and bring it up again in the centre of the next stitch to the left. Repeat this process until you come to the end of the first line to be worked.

Photograph 4

You now have the first line of Swiss darning covered and will need to turn so that you can begin the second row to be worked. After the last stitch on the first row has been covered, bring up the needle into the centre of that stitch.

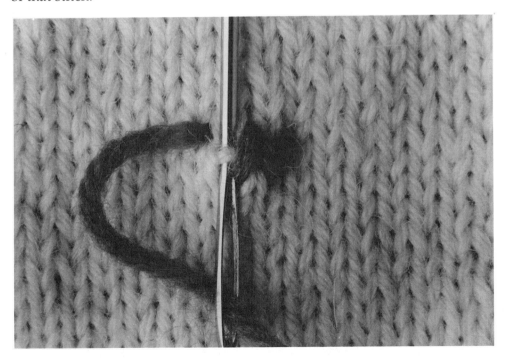

Photograph 5

Now insert the needle around the back of the stitch just above the one to be covered and then back into the stitch below, where it emerged. Bring the needle up again in the centre of the next stitch to the right. Continue repeating until you come to the end of the second row. Then repeat the movements shown in photographs 1, 2 and 3.

Photograph 6

To make a vertical line, begin at the top of the motif. Make one stitch and bring up the needle for the next stitch through the stitch below. Repeat to the bottom of the motif.

❖ ❖ ❖ ❖
Using Charts

There is one very important thing to remember when you are working from a chart that has been especially prepared for embroidery (like cross stitch or tapestry graphs) where each stitch represents a square: the knitted surface is *not* like the embroidery surface. The design will often come out longer and narrower than it would be if it were worked on an embroidery canvas or an ordinary woven surface. When working from such charts, which have not been especially prepared for knitting, make a tension measurement and add extra rows or stitches of Swiss darning to compensate for this distortion.

Helpful Hint

● There is a wide selection of very special knitters' graph paper on the market. This will help you design your own motifs to scale. I strongly advise that beginners should stick to these.

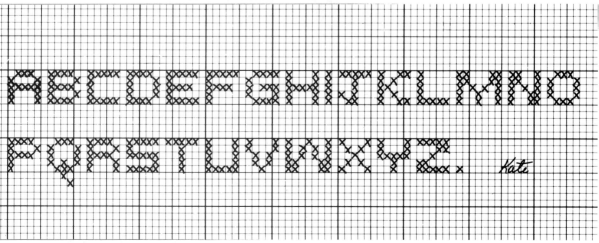

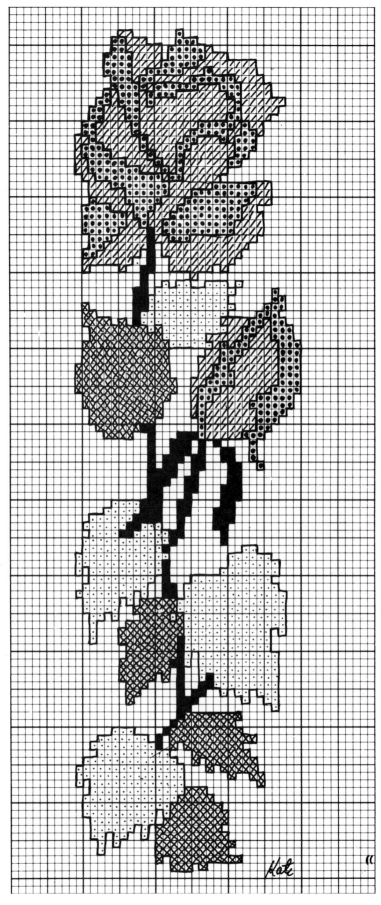

Colour Code

⊠ = MossGreen 406   ■ = Mustard 099   ◿ = Flame Red 044

• = Lime Green 75   ⊙ = Light Pink 066

Rowan D.K. Pure New Wool   25g Hanks.

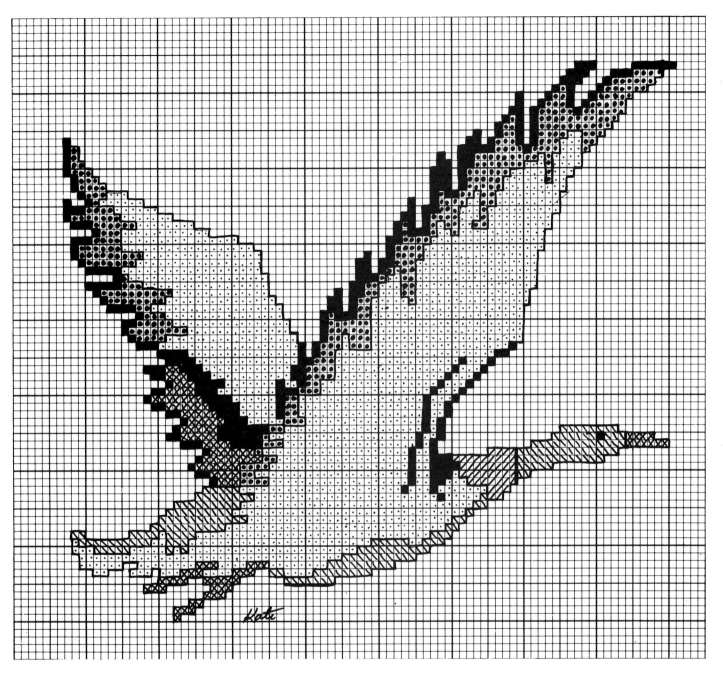

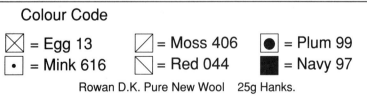

Colour Code

| ⊠ = Egg 13 | ⧄ = Moss 406 | ⬛● = Plum 99 |
| ⊡ = Mink 616 | ⧅ = Red 044 | ⬛ = Navy 97 |

Rowan D.K. Pure New Wool   25g Hanks.

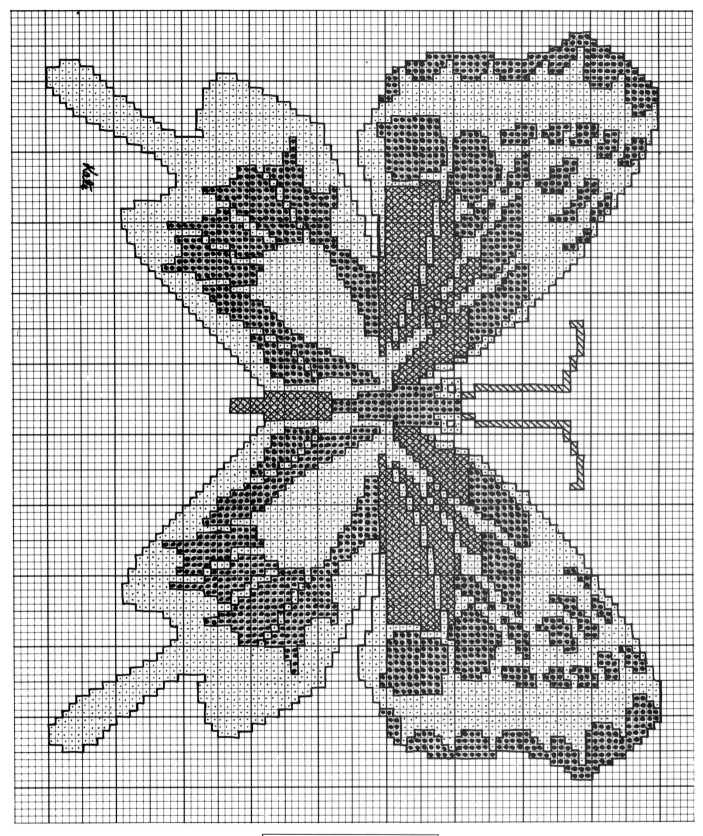

Colour Code

· = Turquoise 125
● = Pink 066
☒ = Purple 126
▨ = Egg 13

❖ ❖ ❖
15. ABBREVIATIONS

The following terms are common to all knitting patterns. It is important to keep a reference like this on hand to save time in translation.

Alt - alternate(ly)

Approx - approximate(ly)

Av - average

B - back

Beg - begin(ning)

CB - centre back

CF - centre front

cm - centimetre(s)

Col - colour

Cont - continue(ing)

Dec - decrease

DK - double knitting

F - front

Foll - following

g. st - garter stitch

in - inch(es)

inc - increase(ing)

K - knit

K wise - insert needle as if to knit

L - left

LH - left hand

M1 - make 1 stitch (by knitting or purling into the one stitch)

MC - main colour

No(s) - number(s)

oz - ounces

P - purl

Patt - pattern

P wise - insert needle as if to purl

PSSO - pass slipped stitch over

Rem - remain(ing)

Rep - repeat

Rev. st st - reverse stocking stitch

R - right

RH - right hand

RS - right side

SKPO - slip 1, knit 1, pass slipped stitch over

SK2PO - slip 2, knit 2 together, pass slipped stitch over

sl - slip

S1K - slip 1 knitwise

S1P - slip 1 purlwise

st - stitch(es)

st st - stocking stitch

TBL - through back of loop(s)

Tog - together

WS - wrong side

YB - yarn back

YF - yarn forward

YON - yarn over needle

YRN - yarn round needle

BASIC CREW NECK SWEATER

Hand Painted and Swiss Darned

SIZES One size only.

TO FIT BUST

ins	34 to 42	
cms	86 to 106	

FINISHED MEASUREMENTS

Width	ins	48
	cms	122
Length	ins	27
	cms	68
Sleeve Length	ins	19
	cms	48

YARN REQUIRED

Tivoli Aranmore 18 x 50g balls. Shade: Natural White 800 (Stockists: Nationwide)

EMBROIDERY YARN

Rowan D.K. pure new wool 1 x 25g hank each colour.
A=cerise 96; B=mid pink 43; C=purple 126; D=lime 75; E=nettle 606; F=moss 406; G=grey 88. (Stockists: Needlecraft, Dawson Street, Dublin 2)

MATERIALS

1 pair each size 4mm and 5mm needles.

INSTRUCTIONS

TENSION

Measured over st st, using 5mm needles, 17 sts x 23 rows = 4 ins (10cm) sq.

NOTES

1. Instructions are given for one size only as this sweater is a unisex fit.
2. Main body of garment is worked in st st (1 row knit, 1 row purl).
3. Yarn amounts are based on average requirements using specific tension and yarn.
4. Motif is hand painted and Swiss Darned after knitting.

BACK

With 4mm needles, cast on 100 sts and work 10 rows in 1 x 1 rib. Change to 5mm needles and work in st st until garment measures 27 inches from beginning. Leave 36 sts for each shoulder on 2 separate stitch holders, and 28 sts for back neck on a 3rd holder.

FRONT

Work as for Back until garment is 18 rows shorter than Back. Begin neck shaping by knitting 41 sts across (on right side row). Place centre 18 sts on a stitch holder for front neck. Now continue working on the 41 sts only at right side of neck. Purl 1 row. Knit following row, decreasing 1 st at neck edge on this row and every following knit row 5 times in all. Work straight to match Back. Leave shoulder stitches on a holder. Reverse shapings on the 41 sts for left side of neck and complete to match first side. Graft left shoulder seam.

NECKBAND

With 4mm needles and beginning at right shoulder, pick up and knit 100 sts all around neck, to include the 18 from front stitch holder and the 28 sts on back stitch holder. Work 10 rows 1 x 1 rib. Cast off.

SLEEVES

With 4mm needles, cast on 42 sts and work 1 x 1 rib for 10 rows. Increase to 60 sts on last rib row. Change to 5mm needles and work in st st, increasing 1 st at each end of every 4th row to 96 sts. Continue straight until sleeve measures 19 inches from beginning. Cast off.

Sew up garment and add knit shoulder pads (see Chapter 11).

HAND PAINTING YOUR GARMENT

PAINTS

Fabric paints in red, yellow and green.
Medium sized watercolour brush. Instructions come with the paints. Place a stiff sheet of cardboard up inside your sweater to stiffen it and make it taut like a canvas. Lay it flat on a table. Keeping to the left side of your garment, using artists' Conté chalk, sketch in tree shapes, some grass etc. Mix red and green and a tiny bit of yellow to give you the tree trunk shade of brown and paint this first. Lay on daubs of green, yellow and red for the foliage etc.
Leave overnight to dry flat.
When completely dry, put a cloth

over it and iron to 'fix' the paints, as the instructions will explain. Embroider floral motif from graph when all this is finished.

N.B. Be extremely careful to use as little water as possible with the paints or the colours will run down the grain of the knitting. Have some tissues nearby just in case you make any mistakes.

Colour Code

◹ = Grey	⊠ = Pink	⊡ = Moss	■ = Lime Green
◿ = Purple	⬤ = Cerise	⊙ = Nettle Green	

'BOLD FLOWERS' SWEATER DRESS

SIZES: One size only

TO FIT BUST

ins	34 to 44
cms	86 to 112

FINISHED MEASUREMENTS

Width	ins	50
	cms	127
Length	ins	34
	cms	86
Sleeve Length	ins	16 1/2
	cms	42

YARN REQUIRED

Tivoli Aranmore 20 x 50g. balls. Shade, Mink 828 (Stockists. Nationwide)
Embroidery yarn
Rowan D.K. Pure new wool 1 x 25g. hank each colour.
A=red 044, B=yellow 12, C=egg 13, D=salmon 22, E=cerise 96, F=mid pink 43, G=light pink 066, H=dark green 124, I=mid green 90, J=light green 89.
(Stockists: Needlecraft, Dawson St, Dublin 2. - Mail Order also)

MATERIALS

1 pair each size: 3mm, 4mm and 5mm needles.

INSTRUCTIONS
TENSION

Measured over stocking stitch, using 5mm needles, 17 sts x 23 rows = 4 ins (10cm) sq.

NOTES

1 Instructions are given for one size only as this style is a generous fit.
2 Main body of this garment is worked in stocking stitch (1 row knit, 1 row purl).
3 Yarn amounts are based on average requirements using specific tension and yarn.
4 Motif is Swiss Darned after knitting.

BACK

Using 4mm needles and Aranmore yarn, cast on 96 sts and work in K1, P1 rib for 1 inch. Change to 5mm needles and knit 40 rows in st st. Change to 3mm needles and work in K1, P1 rib for 2 inches. Change back to 5mm needles and continue in st st for 120 rows. Put sts on 3 holders, 34 sts for each shoulder on separate holders and 28 sts for centre back neck.

FRONT

Work as for Back, but instead of 120 rows st st, work 100 rows and shape crew neck as follows...
Neck shaping: Put centre 16 sts on holder for front centre neck. Cast off 1 st at neck edge on every right side row 6 times and then continue straight until work is same length as Back to shoulders. Put sts on holders for shoulders, 34 sts each side.

SLEEVES

Cast on 45 sts using 4mm needles and work in K1, P1 rib for 5 inches. Increase in every stitch (by knitting twice into each st) on the last rib row to 90 sts. Change to 5mm needles and knit 65 rows in st st. Cast off.

FINISHING

Graft left shoulder seam.

NECKBAND

With 4mm needles, pick up 82 sts all around neck, beginning at right front neck, working around front of neck, to include sts on holder, around to sts on back neck holder. Work K1, P1 rib for 3 inches. Cast off and double down.

FINISHING

Graft right shoulder, set in sleeves, sew up side seams. Steam press body (omitting all ribs). Embroider motifs from graph.
Large graph design is placed on front panel of dress. The smaller repeat 'Rose' pattern travels around base of peblum panel.

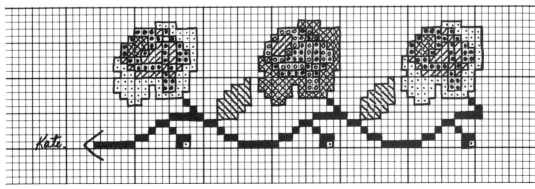

Colour Code

•	= Egg	◡	= Light Pink	■	= Dark Green	⊠	= Red	╱	= Cerise
●	= Yellow	◹	= Mid Green	—	= Light Green	◉	= Salmon	‖	= Mid Pink

❖ ❖ ❖ ❖
'NAVAJO INDIAN'
ETHNIC WAISTCOAT

SIZES One size only

TO FIT BUST

ins	34 to 44
cms	86 to 112

FINISHED MEASUREMENTS

Width	ins	44
	cms	112
Length	ins	17
	cms	43

YARN REQUIRED
Tivoli Killowen D.K. 8 x 50g balls. Shade. Black 100 (Stockists: Nationwide).

CONTRAST COLOURS AND EMBROIDERY YARNS
Rowan D.K. Pure new wool 1 x 25g hank each colour.
A=red 044; B=royal 57; C=moss 406; D=mustard 009; E=egg 13; F=yellow 12, (Stockist: Needlecraft, (Mail Order also) Dawson Street, Dublin 2).

MATERIALS
1 each size 3¼mm and 4mm circular needle.
3.50 crochet hook. 8 tiny (shirt size) buttons in yellow.

INSTRUCTIONS
TENSION
Measured over st st, using 4mm needles, 21 sts x 29 rows = 4 ins (10cm) sq.

NOTES
1 Instructions are given for one size only as this waistcoat is a generous fit.
2 Main body worked in stocking stitch (1 row knit, 1 row purl).
3 Yarn amounts are based on average requirements.
4 Motif is Swiss Darned on after knitting.

GARMENT
Knit all in one piece to armhole.

BODY
With 3¼mm circular needle and black, cast on 232 sts and work in K2, P2 rib for 4 rows. Change to contrasts and work as follows... K2A, P2B for 4 rows; then K2C, P2D for 4 rows; K2E, P2F for 4 rows. (This is called an 'Indian Rib'. Instructions read for the right side only. On wrong side of garment, they will read P2A, K2B; P2C, K2D; P2E, K2F etc.) Change to 4mm needles and black yarn and work 50 rows in st st, then begin neck and armhole shaping.

ARMHOLE
With right side facing work 58 sts (for front right hand side). Turn, cast off 8 sts at beginning of next row and purl to end. *At the same time,* cast off 1 st at neck edge on every right side row. Cast off 4 more sts at armhole edge, then 2 sts at armhole edge, then 1 st at armhole edge on next 2 following right side rows. Continue decreasing at the same time at neck edge until 22 sts are on needle. Then work straight until 110 rows of st st have been worked in all since rib. Cast off. Work the second front the same, *but* reverse shapings. Then finally work the 116 sts for back, decreasing 8 sts at beg of next 2 rows, 4 sts at beg of next 2 rows, 1 st at each end of next 2 right side rows, finish to match fronts in length. Cast off.

BANDS
Sew up shoulder seams.

ARMHOLES
Using 3.50 crochet hook and black yarn, work 1 row of double crochet all around armholes, then 1 row A; 1 row B; 1 row black.

FRONT BANDS
Using 3.50 crochet hook and beginning at side of left front rib, with black yarn, work 2 rows of double crochet (up left front, across back neck and down right side). Now work up and down left front only and not across back neck. Work 1 row A; 1 row B, and now begin fancy Bohemian crochet pattern by working 2 stitches C, 2 sts D for 2 rows; then 2 sts E and 2 sts F for 2 rows. Do the same with the right front after left one is completed. This means you have 2 wide fancy fronts, but only a thin black border across back neck. Work 1 row B, 1 row A, 1 row Black to complete. On button band sew the 8 tiny buttons onto first band when finished and work chain crochet loops on opposite band to correspond with buttons, in the final row of black double crochet. (Button loops, 5 chain and fasten down onto band in exact same stitch as chain started, to form a loop).

FINISHING
Embroider motifs from graphs.

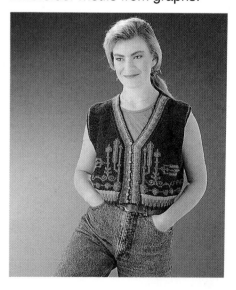

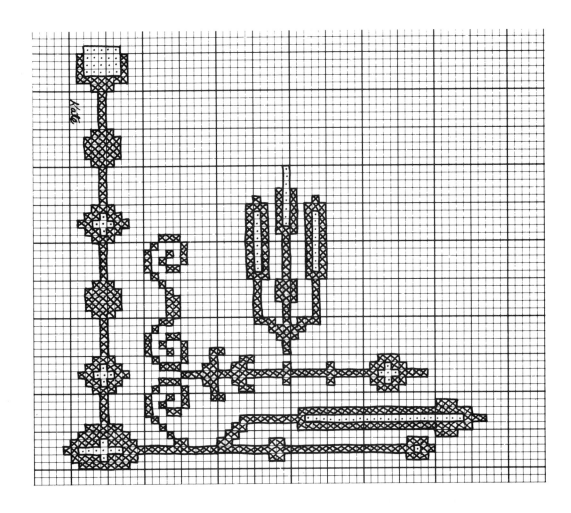

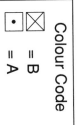

Colour Code

⊠ = B
· = A

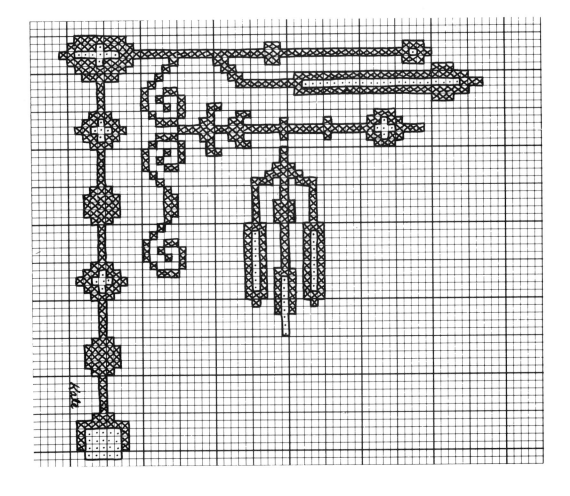

'ACOUSTIC GUITAR' WAISTCOAT

SIZES   One size only.

TO FIT BUST

ins		36 to 48
cms		91 to 122

FINISHED MEASUREMENTS

Width	ins	54
	cms	137
Length	ins	28 1/2
	cms	72

TENSION

Measured over stocking stitch, using 4mm needles, 21 sts x 29 rows = 4 ins (10cms) sq. (see Chapter 'Tension')

NOTES

1   Instructions are given for one size only as this waistcoat is a generous fit.
2   Main body worked in stocking stitch (1 row knit, 1 row purl).
3   Yarn amounts are based on average requirements.
4   Motif is Swiss Darned on after knitting (see Chapter on Swiss Darning).

MATERIALS

Tivoli Killowen Superwash D.K. x 50g balls. Approx 4 balls black 100; 4 balls golden glory 838; 2 balls bracken 807; 2 balls cobalt 921; 2 balls caribbean 646. Embroidery. Rowan D.K. pure new wool 1 hank x 25g each colour. (Stockist: Needlecraft, Dawson Street, Dublin 2.) A=red 044; B=white; C=light grey 60, 1 each size 3¼ and 4mm circular needles. Crochet hook size 3.50. 10 yellow buttons.

BODY

With 3¼. circular needle, cast on 256 sts with black yarn and work K2, P2 rib for 4 rows. Then commence Indian Rib by working thus... K2 cobalt, P2 caribbean for 4 rows. K2 caribbean, P2 cobalt for 4 rows. K2 cobalt, P2 caribbean for 4 rows. On wrong side rows, this will read: P2 cobalt, K2 caribbean for 4 rows; P2 caribbean, K2 cobalt for 4 rows; P2 cobalt, K2 caribbean for 4 rows etc.

Change to 4mm needles and work 46 rows golden glory in stocking stitch, then 12 rows in bracken, then 16 rows cobalt, 14 rows caribbean, 10 rows black and then begin to shape armholes. With right side facing and commencing at left front, knit 64 sts and turn, cast off 10 sts at beg of next row and purl to end. Decrease 1 st at beginning of next row (for slope of neck edge), dec 4 sts at *armhole edge* on next row (while still dec 1 st at neck edge), and 4 sts more at armhole edge on following row. Continue as set decreasing at neck edge all the time 1 stitch and then dec 1 st at armhole edge on next 3 purl rows. Continue decreasing now at neck edge only until 24 sts on needle, work

straight until 90 rows of black in all. Cast off.

Reverse shapings for right side and then work across 128 sts of back, decreasing at armhole edges as on fronts. Cast off. Sew shoulders to back.

ARMHOLE BANDS

With 3.50 crochet hook, work 1 row black, 1 row caribbean, 1 row cobalt, 1 row black, in double crochet stitch.

FRONTS

Beginning at bottom of left front, work 2 rows black, (across back neck, down right front and back again to bottom of left front). Now continue to work on left front only and work... 1 row cobalt, 1 row caribbean, and then fancy Bohemian crochet design of 4 stitches golden glory, 4 sts bracken in double crochet for 2 rows, then 4 bracken, 4 golden glory for 2 rows. Then 1 row caribbean, 1 row cobalt and 1 row black to complete. On right side work 10 button loops with 5 chain stitch fastened down to the band for each loop.

Embroider guitar and desert scene motif onto both fronts of the waistcoat from graphs.

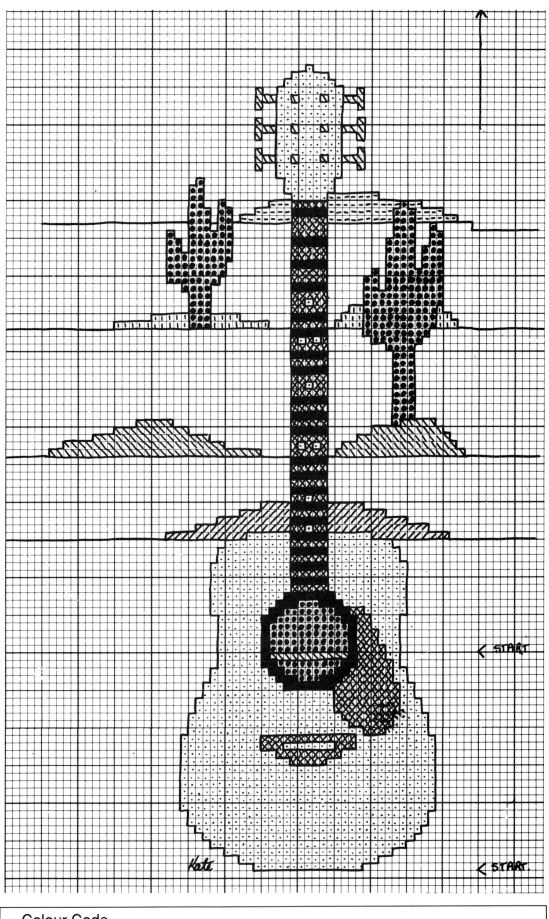

❖ ❖ ❖ ❖
'WILD FLOWER' WAISTCOAT

SIZES   One size only

TO FIT BUST

ins		34 to 44
cms		86 to 112

FINISHED MEASUREMENTS

Width	ins		44
	cms		112
Length	ins		17
	cms		43

YARN REQUIRED

Tivoli Superwash Killowen D.K. x 50g. balls. 4 balls shade: nephin 705, 2 balls shade French grey 621, 2 balls shade Mink 828. (Stockists: Nationwide). Contrast colours and embroidery shades. Rowan D.K. Pure new wool 1 x 25g. hank each colour
A=red 044, B=mid pink 43, C=mustard 099, D=bright orange 646, E=egg 13, F=chestnut 77.
Stockists: Needlecraft, Dawson St., Dublin 2.

MATERIALS

1 size 3 1/4mm and 4mm circular needles.
3.50 crochet hook.
7 medium sized yellow buttons.

INSTRUCTIONS

TENSION

Measured over st st, using 4mm needles, 21 sts x 29 rows = 4 inches (10cm) sq.

NOTES

1   Instructions are given for one size only as this waistcoat is a generous fit.
2.   Main body worked in st st (1 row knit, 1 row purl).
3.   Yarn amounts are based on average requirements.
4.   Motif is Swiss Darned after knitting.

GARMENT

Knit all in one piece to armhole.

BODY

With 3 1/4mm needle and nephin shade, cast on 232 sts and work in K1, P2 rib for 4 rows. Change to contrasts and work as follows...
K2E, P2F for 4 rows; then K2C, P2D for 4 rows; then K2A, P2B for 4 rows. (This is called an 'Indian Rib'.) On wrong side of work, this rib will read: P2E, K2F for 4 rows ... etc.
Change to 4mm needles and nephin shade and work 50 rows in st st, then begin neck and armhole shaping. Change to mink shade for the next 30 rows, then finally grey.

ARMHOLE

With right side facing, work 58 sts (for front right hand side). Turn, cast off 8 sts at beg next row and purl to end. *At the same time*, cast off 1 st at neck edge on every right side row. Cast off 4 sts more at armhole edge, then 2 sts at armhole edge, then 1 st at armhole edge on next 2 following right side rows. Continue decreasing at the same time at neck edge until 22 sts on needle. Work straight until 110 rows of st st worked since rib.

Cast off.
Work the second front the same, but reverse shapings. Then finally work the 116 sts for Back, decreasing 8 sts at beg next 2 rows, 4 sts at beg next 2 rows, 1 st at each end of next 2 right side rows. Finish to match fronts in length. Cast off.

BANDS

Sew up shoulder seams.

ARMHOLES

Using 3.50 crochet hook and mink yarn, work 1 row of double crochet all around armholes, then 1 row A; 1 row orange; 1 row mink.

FRONT BANDS

Using 3.50 crochet hook and beg at side of left front rib with mink yarn, work 2 rows double crochet (up left front, across back neck and down right side). Now work up and down left front only and not across back neck. Do the same with right front after left one is completed. This means you have 2 wide fancy front borders, but only a thin mink border across back neck. Now begin fancy Bohemian crochet pattern by working: 1 row E; 1 row C; 2 sts A, 2 sts orange

for 4 rows; 1 row B; 1 row F; 1 row mink.
On button band sew the 7 buttons onto the first band when it is finished and work chain crochet loops (5 chain and fasten down onto band in exact same stitch as chain started) on the opposite band to correspond with the buttons, in the final row of mink double crochet.

FINISHING

Embroider motifs from graphs.

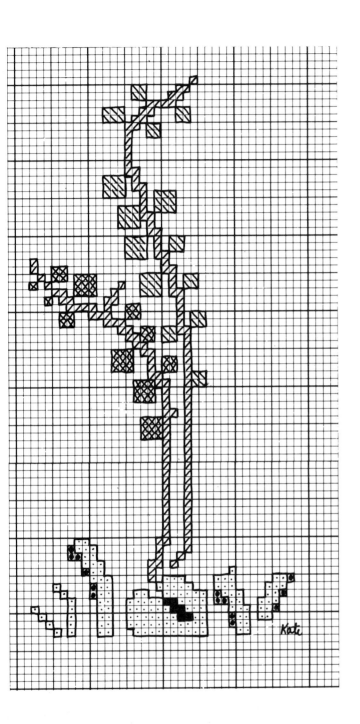

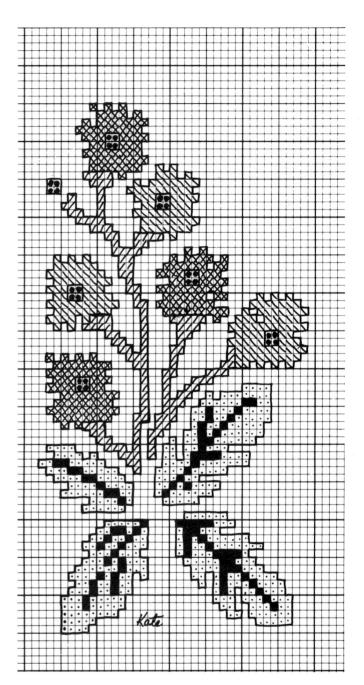

Colour Code

■ = Chestnut   ⊠ = Red   ⧄ = Orange

• = Egg   ● = Mid Pink   ⧄ = Mustard

❖❖❖❖
'PIANO' WAISTCOAT

SIZES One size only.

TO FIT BUST

ins	36 to 48
cms	91 to 122

FINISHED MEASUREMENTS

Width	ins	54
	cms	137
Length	ins	28 1/2
	cms	72

TENSION
Measured over stocking stitch, using 4mm needles, 21 sts x 29 rows = 4 ins (10cms) sq. (see Chapter 'Tension')

NOTES
1 Instructions are given for one size only as this waistcoat is a generous fit.
2 Main body worked in stocking stitch (1 row knit, 1 row purl).

3 Yarn amounts are based on average requirements.
4 Motif is Swiss Darned on after knitting (see Chapter on Swiss Darning).

MATERIALS
Tivoli Killowen Superwash D.K. x 50g balls, approx 8 balls Cobalt 921, 1 ball Cherry 814, 1 ball Black 100, 1 ball White 300.
3 1/4 and 4mm circular needles. 3.50 crochet hook. 4 large buttons.

GARMENT
Knit all in one piece to armholes.
With 3¼mm needles, cast on 256 sts in cobalt and work K2, P2 rib for 4 rows. Commence Indian Rib as follows... K2 cobalt, P2 cherry, for 4 rows; then K2 black, P2 white for 8 rows. On wrong side rows, this pattern will work in reverse: P2 cobalt, K2 cherry for 4 rows etc.
Change to 4mm needles and work 2 rows st st in white, then 98 rows st st in cobalt, to armholes.
Armhole shaping (right side facing): Commencing at left front, knit 64 sts and turn, cast off 10 sts at beg of next row and purl to end. Decrease 1 st at beg of next row (for slope of neck edge); dec 4 sts at armhole edge on next 2 purl rows, while still dec 1 st at neck edge on every knit row, dec 1 st at armhole edge on next 3 purl rows then continue decreasing at neck edge only until 24 sts on needle. Work straight until 178 rows of st st in all have been worked after rib. Cast off.
Reverse shapings for right front, then work across 128 sts for Back, decreasing at armholes only on Back. Sew shoulders to back.

ARMHOLE BANDS
With 3.50 crochet hook, work 2 rows cobalt, 1 row cherry, 1 row white, 1 row cobalt in double crochet stitch.

FRONT BANDS
Beg at bottom of left front, work 2 rows cobalt (across back neck,

down right front, and back again to bottom of left front). Now work 1 row red; then 3 sts in white, 3 sts in black, in double crochet sts for 2 rows; then 1 row cherry all around bands to finish.

EMBROIDERY
Starting at top of shoulders, work small keyboards motif down right front in black and white as chart, and smaller motifs in red underneath. Starting at left shoulder, work larger keyboards motif down left front in black and white from chart and smaller notes motif just above rib in black.
See Charts. The keyboards motif may also be repeated down the 2 shoulders at the back of the waistcoat.

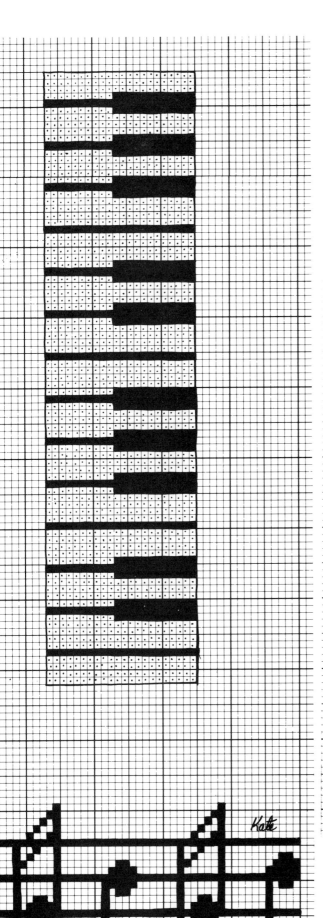

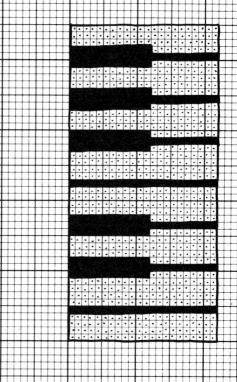

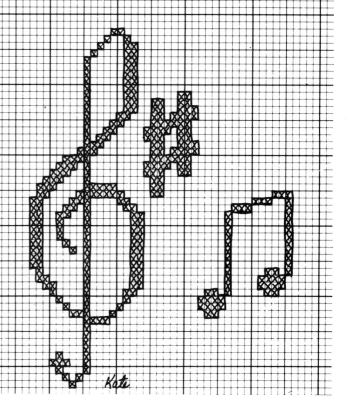

PEBLUM TAPESTRY JACKET

SIZES
To fit bust

ins	32 to 34	34 to 36	36 to 38
cms	81 to 86	86 to 91	91 to 96

ACTUAL MEASUREMENTS

Width	ins	40	42	44
	cms	101	107	112
Length	ins	24	24	24
	cms	61	61	61
Sleeve	ins	17½	18	19
Length	cms	44	45½	48

MATERIALS
Tivoli Aranmore x

50g balls	18 balls	18 balls	19 balls

Shade Navy 821

EMBROIDERY YARN
Rowan D.K. pure new wool 1 x 25g hank of each colour.
A=moss 406, B=mustard 009, C=red 044, D=cherry 43, E=wine 067.

NEEDLES
1 pair each size 3³/4mm, 4¹/2mm and 5mm needles. 2.50mm crochet hook. 8 moss green buttons.

TENSION
Measured over stocking stitch, using 4¹/2mm needles, 20 sts x 24 rows = 4 ins (10cm) sq. Knit a tension square. If too small use larger needles; if too large use smaller needles.

NOTES
1. Instructions are given for second size. Figures in () brackets refer to smaller and larger sizes. When only one figure is given, this applies to all sizes.
2. Yarn amounts are based on average requirements using specific yarn and tension.
3. Main body of garment is worked in st st. (1 row knit, 1 row purl).
4. Responsibility cannot be accepted for the finished garment if yarn other than Tivoli is used.
5. Motif is Swiss Darned onto finished garment.

BACK
Using 4¹/2mm needles, cast on (123), 133, (143) sts and work in moss stitch for 9cm (3½ins). **Moss Stitch** Pattern repeats over 2 rows and an uneven number of sts. Cast on sts (uneven no.) **1st row.** *K1, P1, rep from * to end. **2nd row.** Purl where knit sts are and knit where purl sts are.

Dec row. Work 8 sts, work 2 tog, work 3 sts, work 2 tog to last 10 sts, work 2 tog, work 8 sts. (99), 109, (119) sts.
Change to 3³/4mm needles and work 8 rows in K1, P1 rib, starting with a purl st, then a knit one. Change to 4¹/2mm needles and work in st st until work measures 26¹/2 cm (10¹/2ins) from top of rib.

SHAPE ARMHOLES
With right side facing, cast off 6 sts at beg of next 2 rows, then dec 1 st at each end of next 3 rows, and 1 st at each end of following alternate row. (77), 87, (97) sts remain.
Work straight to 49¹/2cm (19¹/2ins) from top of rib.

SHAPE SHOULDERS
Cast off (22), 29, (32) sts at beg of next 2 rows. Put remaining (23), 29, (33) sts on holder for neck.

RIGHT FRONT
With 4¹/2mm needles cast on (62), 67, (72) sts and work in moss stitch as on Back.
Dec row. Work 5 sts, work 2 tog, work 3 sts, work 2 tog, to last 7 sts, work 2 tog, work 5 sts. (50), 55, (60) sts.
Change to 3³/4mm needles and work 8 rows in K1, P1 rib, beginning with a purl stitch. Change to 4¹/2mm needles and work in st st until work measures same as Back to armhole shaping.

With wrong side facing, cast off 6 sts, dec 1 st at armhole edge on next 3 rows, then 1 st at armhole edge on next 2 alternate rows. (39), 44, (49) sts. Continue in st st until work measures 12 rows less than Back.

NECK DECREASING
Cast off 8 sts at neck edge, work 1 row, cast off 4 sts, work 1 row. Decrease 1 st on next 3 alt rows. (24), 29, (34) sts. Work until the same amount of rows as Back are completed. Cast off remaining sts.

LEFT FRONT
Work as for Right Front, but reverse all shapings.

SLEEVES
With 3³/4mm needles, cast on (44), 48, (54) sts and work in Twisted Rib for 9cm (3¹/2ins). **Twisted Rib** Pattern repeats over 1 row and an even number of sts. **1st row** *K2, P2, rep from * to end of row.
2nd row and every alternate row. Knit where knit sts are and purl where purl sts are. **3rd row** (on knit ridge) *knit second stitch of knit ridge first, then knit first st and pull both off needle together. Purl 2, repeat from * to end of row. Work all knit ridges on the right side rows in this manner and leave all purl sts to be purled as usual.
Increase 21 sts on last row (65), 69, (75) sts. Change to 4¹/2mm needles and work in moss stitch, inc 1 stitch at each end of 7th row and every following 10th row to (80), 85, (90) sts.
Cast off 6 sts at beg of next 2 rows. Cast off 1 st at each end of next 5 alternate rows, then 1 st at each end of every row until (18), 23, (28) sts remain. Cast off 4 sts on next 2 rows,

cast off 3 sts on next 2 rows. Cast off remaining sts.

MAKE UP
Join shoulder seams.

NECKBAND
With right side facing and using 3³/4mm needles, pick up 23 sts from right front neck, take in sts from back neck and pick up 23 sts down left front neck. Work 4 rows in moss stitch. Cast off.

FRONT BANDS
(both the same)
With right side facing and using 3³/4mm needles, pick up 109 sts along front edge and work 4 rows in moss stitch. Cast off.

CROCHET BUTTON LOOPS
With 2.50mm crochet hook and starting on left side at bottom of moss panel on the right side of the garment, work 3 doubles, 4 chain (skip 3 sts), 10 doubles, 4 chain (skip 3 sts), 10 doubles, etc. to neck. Work 8 buttonholes. If you are unable to work the crochet loops, use a large darning needle and make 8 loops with the wool every 2¹/2ins from bottom of garment on the band.

KNIT SHOULDER PADS
Using 5mm needle work 38 sts and 40 rows in K1, P1 rib. Fold the square into a triangle and sew point to neck and wide base across top of sleeve, centering across shoulder line.
Set in sleeves by placing centre of cast off edge to shoulder seam and back stitch from shoulder to underarm. Join side and sleeve seams. Sew in all loose threads.

Colour Code

■ = Moss	● = Cherry	☒ = Wine	
◩ = Mustard	⋅ = Red		

❖ ❖ ❖ ❖
'WILD HERON' JACKET

SIZES One size only.

TO FIT BUST
ins	34 to 44
cms	86 to 112

FINISHED MEASUREMENTS
Width	ins	50
	cms	127
Length	ins	30
	cms	76
Sleeves	ins	17
Length	cms	43

YARN REQUIRED
Tivoli Aranmore x 50g balls. 20 balls, shade 505 Saltee (Stockists: Nationwide)

EMBROIDERY YARN
Rowan pure new wool 1 x 25g hank each colour.
A=97 navy; B=white; C=066 pink; D=12 yellow; E=13 egg; F=75 lime; G=606 nettle; H=009 mustard; I=125 turquoise. Stockist: Needlecraft, Dawson Street, Dublin 2.

MATERIALS
9 mustard yellow buttons, 1 pair each size 4mm and 5mm needles.

TENSION
Measured over st st, using 5mm needles, 17 sts x 23 rows = 4 ins (10cm) sq.

NOTES
1   Instructions are given for one size only as this jacket is a generous fit.
2   Main body of garment is worked in stocking stitch (1 row knit, 1 row purl).
3   Yarn amounts are based on average requirements using specific tension and yarn.
4   Motif is Swiss Darned after knitting (see Chapter on Swiss Darning).

BACK
With 4mm needles cast on 108 sts and work in K1, P1 rib for 4 inches. Change to 5mm needles and work in st st (1 row knit, 1 row purl) until work measures 30 inches. Cast off.

POCKETS
(make 2)
With 5mm needles cast on 30 sts and work 35 rows in st st. Put stitches on holder.

LEFT FRONT
With 4mm needles, cast on 50 sts and work in K1, P1 rib for 4 inches. Change to 5mm needles and work 40 rows in st st. Knit 10 sts, put centre 30 sts onto a holder and knit the 30 sts of the pocket in their place, then knit remaining 10 sts. Continue in st st until work is 15 rows less than Back.

NECK SHAPING
With right side facing, cast off 8 sts, knit 1 row, decrease 2 sts at neck edge on every right side row, 3 times. Continue straight until work measures same as Back. Cast off.

RIGHT FRONT
Work as for Left Front, reversing all shapings.

SLEEVES
With 4mm needles cast on 48 sts and work in K1, P1 rib for 4 inches, increasing 10sts evenly along last row (58) sts. Change to 5mm needles and work 6 rows in st st, increasing 1 st at each end of next and every following 6th row to 76 sts. Work straight until sleeve measures 18 inches. Cast off.

BUTTONBAND
With 4mm needles, cast on 10 sts and work in K1, P1 rib until band measures from beginning of rib to beginning of neck shaping. Leave stitches on holder.

BUTTONHOLE BAND
Work as for Buttonband for 1 inch.
Next row With right side facing, fix pocket ribs to front to secure neatly. Rib 4, cast off 2 sts, rib 4.
Next row With wrong side facing rib 4, cast on 2 sts, rib 4. Work a further 8 buttonholes approx 3 inches apart.

NECKBAND
Join shoulder seams. With right side facing, pick up 10 sts from buttonhole band, 20 sts up right front neck, 34 sts across back, 20 sts down left neck edge, 10 sts buttonband. (94 sts). Work in K1, P1 rib and insert 9th buttonhole after 1 inch, work 1 inch, make another buttonhole. This will fall behind 9th buttonhole when neck is doubled down and sewn on the inside. Cast off loosely in rib.

POCKETS TOPS
With 4mm needles work 6 rows in K1, P1 rib. Cast off.

HOULDER PADS
With 7mm needles, cast on 38 sts and work in K1, P1 rib for 40 rows. Fold square into triangle and sew down. Sew point to neck and wide end to shoulder seam.

MAKE UP
Fold neckband in half and slip stitch to inside. Sew in sleeves. Sew front bands onto jacket and sew up side and sleeve seams. Sew up pockets to inside of jacket.

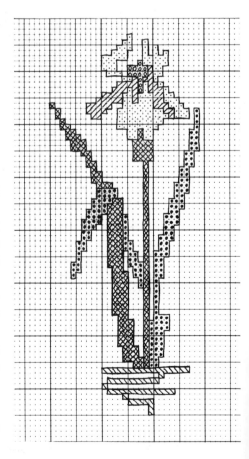

Colour Code

● = Nettle   • = Yellow   ⧅ = Egg   ⊃ = Salmon   ■ = Navy

⊠ = Lime   ⊙ = Mustard   — = White | = Red   ⧄ = Turquoise

❖ ❖ ❖ ❖
PAINTING ON KNITWEAR

One of the most creative ways of decorating your own knitwear is by using fabric dye paints. Brush on, stencil or spray - many techniques are possible. The paints are non-toxic and waterbased. When fixed by ironing, they are colourfast, machine washable and can also be dry cleaned. The paints usually come in small paint jars with instructions for use on the label.

There is a marvellous selection of colours on the market. They include twenty standard shades for light-coloured fabrics, nine sparkling shades for light and dark fabrics, twelve high-density shades for dark fabrics, and six 'neon' shades for light fabrics (these react to ultra violet light).

It is a good idea to select an 'outlining liquid' to draw on your design first. This will stop the colours from smudging and will help to contain the painted shape. You can usually choose from three types of outlining liquids - colourless, gold or silver. These come in plastic bottles. You pierce the top of the bottle and then use it like a pencil or marker by holding it upright while working. When the outlining liquid is dry, dip your brush into the chosen colour of paint and start in the middle of the motif, letting the colour flow out to reach the outline. Then just let it dry and iron it.

Always put a piece of stiff cardboard inside your sweater before beginning work. This makes the fabric appear stretched and taut like canvas on a stretcher. Leave this board inside during work, drying and ironing. Never stand the garment upright while working or the dyes may run down the grain of the knitting. French Conté chalk, which can be bought in any artists' suppliers, is the best for outlining the motif as it holds on the rough knitwear surface longer than any other chalk.

If you want to achieve the softer edges of a watercolour painting technique, all you need is a smooth watercolour brush (I find Chinese bamboo brushes or sable hair brushes are best) and some cotton wool buds. Apply the paint to your design. While it is still wet, dip the cotton wool bud into water and apply it to make the colour lighter in selected areas. This method is particularly effective on silk or cotton garments.